GOURD PYROGRAPHY

Jim Widess

Sterling Publishing Co., Inc.
New York

Designed by Judy Morgan
Edited by Jeanette Green
Photos by Jim Widess unless otherwise noted

Library of Congress Cataloging-in-Publication Data

Widess, Jim.
  Gourd pyrography / Jim Widess.
    p. cm.
  Includes index.
  ISBN 0-8069-5884-7
  1. Gourd craft. 2. Pyrography—Technique. I. Title.

TT873.5 .W54 2002
745.5—dc21   2001057642

3 5 7 9 10 8 6 4 2

Published by Sterling Publishing Company, Inc.
387 Park Avenue South, New York, NY 10016
© 2002 Jim Widess
Distributed in Canada by Sterling Publishing
^c/o Canadian Manda Group
One Atlantic Avenue, Suite 105, Toronto, Ontario, Canada M6K 3E7
Distributed in Australia by Capricorn Link (Australia) Pty. Ltd.
P.O. Box 704, Windsor, NSW 2756 Australia
Printed in China
All rights reserved

ISBN 0-8069-5884-7

Gourd Art Credits

Front cover, top row, left to right: Carousel Rhinoceros back side, Celtic knots, Gary Devine; Swirls, Dic Bonsett; Underwater, Susan Sweet. *Bottom row, left to right:* pear-shaped container, Carol Morrison; Pear-Shaped Sampler, Duane Teeter. *Left jacket flap:* Friendly Advice, Leah Comerford. *Right jacket flap:* Bull, Diane Merrill. *Back cover (from top, clockwise):* Peruvian artist Eulogio Medina; Geometric, Dic Bonsett; Frog, Susan Sweet; Totemic Bird, Susan Sweet.

p. 3: Bull, Diane Merrill. *p. 5 (top to bottom):* Ancient Horse Pitcher, Diane Merrill; Lily and Dogwood Blossoms, Pat Grigg; Mare and Foal, Betty Finch. *p. 6:* Whimsy, Skip Howell. *p. 7 (top):* Carousel Rhinoceros, Gary Devine. *p. 20:* Snake, Glenda McBride. *p. 21 (top):* Geometric, Dic Bonsett. *p. 28:* Maile and Mokihana Ipu, Nicole DuPont. *p. 29:* Leaves, Dic Bonsett,.

p. 144: small apple-shaped container with lid, Gretchen Ceteras.

Ancient House Pitcher, Diane Merrill

Lily and Dogwod Blossoms, Pat Grigg

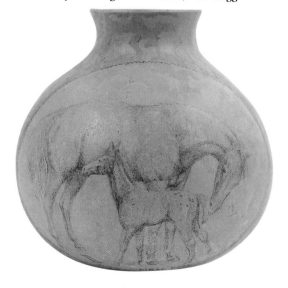

Mare and Foal, Betty Finch

CONTENTS

Gourd pyrography, heat engraving, has been popular in all parts of the world and practiced for centuries.

INTRODUCTION TO PYROGRAPHY

𝒫yrography is the art of using fire to draw, carve, or scorch on wood, paper, or fabric. The word *pyrography* comes from *pyro*, which means "fire," and *graphy*, which means "writing." The art of gourd pyrography can be found all over the world from Africa to Asia to South and Central America to the South Pacific Islands and to North America and Europe.

Perhaps as a child you used a soldering iron or another type of device to burn a preprinted design on a flat piece of wood to create a plaque or box, maybe as a gift for your parents. If you did this at camp, at home, in art class, or in shop at school, you probably used a tool hot enough to give you a nasty burn. You may have found it difficult to adjust the temperature of the tool, to govern the consistency of the burned line, or indeed to have any real control over the bulky tool. You couldn't really get your hand close enough to the work to do any fancy writing. Usually, after one unsuccessful attempt, you may have given up and never burned again. If you were working at home, you may still have that tool hidden away in storage.

Cross with four fields and symbols; checkerboard patterns on gourd from Ghana.

Dick and Beanie Wezelman collection

In the 1980s and 1990s, engineers greatly improved pyrography tools. Now at least six companies manufacture solid-state, wood-burning systems with variable-temperature power supplies. Most have dozens of different tips for use as burning pens that provide the perfect edge for undercutting duck bills, shaping fish or snake scales, and creating fine detail work on feathers. Some tips are even designed for left-handers. If there's a tip you want that doesn't exist, these manufacturers will custom design it for you.

But don't give up yet on that tool from your childhood. As you'll see in these pages, if you have a steady hand and an open mind, you can figure out ways to make that old tool come to life.

Many ancient pyrography traditions continue and many artists bring original inspiration to the art. In this chapter, we've collected examples of gourd pyrography created after 1900 from working artists in Nigeria, Kenya, Mali, Ghana, Senegal, China, Peru, Mexico, New Guinea, and the South Pacific Islands. In later chapters you'll learn the techniques of artists all over the world and perhaps discover a few near home.

In Nigeria, Kenya, and Mali, artists use many heavy, iron needles for pyrography. When ready to work, the artist places them in an open fire for heating. When she needs a needle, she takes one at a time out of the fire to burn the design. As the needles cool, they are returned to the fire while the artist uses another tool, already preheated, to continue the design.

Tools with a sharp edge carve into the gourd's surface, and other shaped tools are used to fill dark color into the design. Here are many examples from Africa, created by artists from Kenya, Nigeria, Ghana, Senegal, and Mali.

PYROGRAPHY FROM AROUND THE WORLD

Gourd art is popular in all parts of Africa. Here are examples from Kenya, Mali, Nigeria, Ghana, and Senegal.

AFRICAN GOURDS

Primitive animals and geometric patterns on bowl gourd from Mali. Kathie McDonald collection

Black and sepia-tone crosses on Mali bowl.
Kathie McDonald collection

Bird ornament from Ghana.
Dick and Beanie Wezelman collection

Triangle patterns on gourd from Kenya.
Dick and Beanie Wezelman collection

Circular geometric pattern on round Nigerian gourd. Dick and Beanie Wezelman collection

GOURD PYROGRAPHY

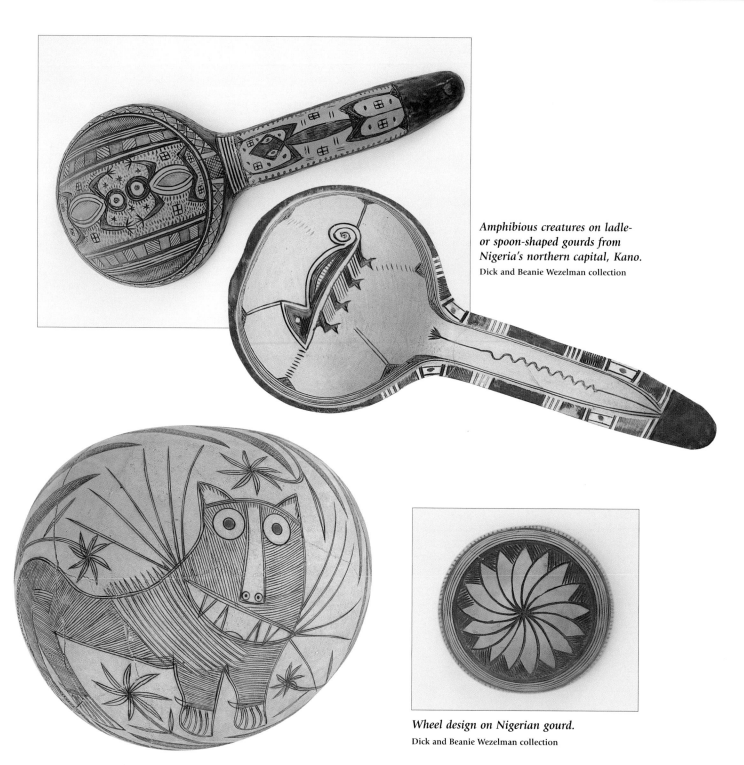

*Amphibious creatures on ladle-
or spoon-shaped gourds from
Nigeria's northern capital, Kano.*
Dick and Beanie Wezelman collection

Cat design from Mali.
Dick and Beanie Wezelman collection

Wheel design on Nigerian gourd.
Dick and Beanie Wezelman collection

GOURD ARTISTS AT WORK

A woman in an artisans' village in Dakar, Senegal, adjusts the fire source when decorating a large bowl-shaped gourd.

Photo by Beanie Wezelman

In Bangu, Nigeria, a Waja pyrography artist shows the broad movements of the technique when applying a border rim design on a large, bowl-shaped gourd.

Photo by Marla C. Berns

Artist Alaja Linga in Borrong, Nigeria, scorches the surface of a Mbula gourd bowl (kwar) and creates a triangular design with striations.

Photos by Marla C. Berns

In New Guinea, in the South Pacific, pyrography artists use the midrib of the sago-palm leaf, stripped of its leaflets and set on fire. Once caught, the artist blows out the flame and brings the glowing ember on the end of the woodlike rib close to the gourd's surface. By blowing on the hot ember, the artist scorches an area of the gourd. The artist "paints" an area with heat on the gourd then carves through the blackened area to create the design.

GOURDS FROM NEW GUINEA

Round gourd lime container from the Trobriand Islands, New Guinea. Dick and Beanie Wezelman collection

Long gourd lime container from the Trobriand Islands, New Guinea. Dick and Beanie Wezelman collection

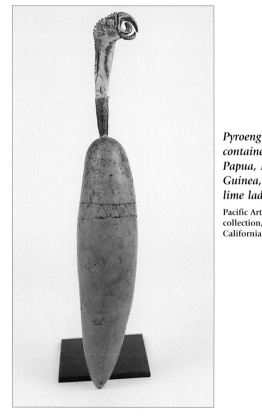

Pyroengraved lime container from Papua, New Guinea, with bone lime ladle.
Pacific Artifacts collection, Vista, California

In the Andean village of Cochas, Peru, Huanca Indians trade for gourds, which are transported 1,000 miles from the arid coast where they're grown. First the gourd artist carves the gourd with a burin, usually without any preliminary sketching. A *burin* is a sharpened nail set into a block of wood for a handle. To color the design, the artist lights a eucalyptus stick with fire. When it's burning well, the artist extinguishes the flame and places the red-hot embers next to the design and blows on the embers to maintain the temperature. The artist can create colors from light tan to reddish brown to black, depending on how close the burning ember is to the gourd's surface and how hard he blows on the embers. Later, to create a bas-relief effect, some of the undecorated gourd surface is chiseled away leaving two surface layers for the foreground and background.

SCORCHED GOURDS FROM PERU

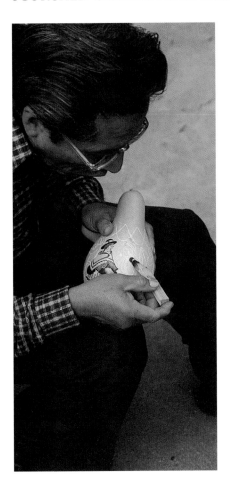  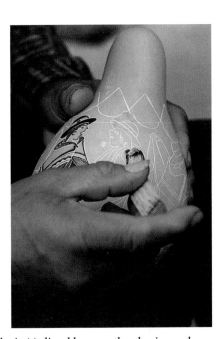

To color the gourd shell, Peruvian artist Eulogio Medina blows on the glowing ember of a stick of wood. When heat scorching, the artist often holds different sizes of sticks to create different temperature burns. Photo by Paul Baumann

Flowers and leaves decorate these gourds.
Author's collection

Musician. On this scorched gourd, lime added to the incised lines creates the white color. Author's collection

GOURDS FROM PERU

Story Gourd. Author's collection

Dancers. Author's collection

Barrette with man, woman, and Llamas. Author's collection

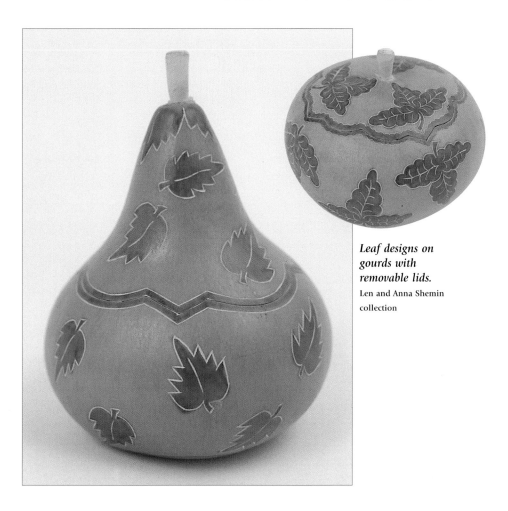

Leaf designs on gourds with removable lids.
Len and Anna Shemin collection

Acorn-shaped gourd with flowers and a removable lid. Len and Anna Shemin collection

Pear-shaped gourd decorated with flowers has a removable lid.
Len and Anna Shemin collection

Llama and cacti. Sher Lynn Elliott-Widess collection

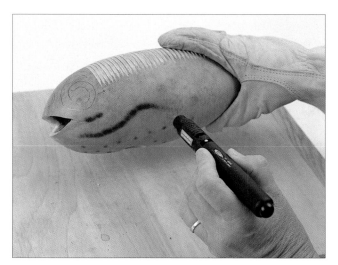

Today many Peruvian artists use mini-butane torches for scorching because of their convenience, like this one used by American artist Ginger Summit.

Chinese Style of Heat Engraving Gourds

In China, gourd pyrography seems to have begun in the 1850s, while burning on paper, silk, palm fronds, and bamboo has a more ancient tradition. Combining the technique of a burning ember and a steel needle, Wang Shixiang was taught to insert a 1-inch (25-mm) length of bicycle spoke into the end of a joss stick.

Wang Shixiang writes, "When using the old method, one has to lift the joss stick and hold the gourd to the height of one's brows, or else smoke will get in his eyes while engraving." The tools he used are a thick joss stick and iron needles.

The Joss Stick

The joss stick is as thick as a finger and about 1 meter (3.3 feet) long and was called bianganzi xiang (whip stick) or ziwu xiang (a joss stick burning from midnight till noon). "It was used to worship god or to drive away mosquitoes... Cut the stick into several pieces, each piece a little longer than a writing brush," Wang writes.

Iron Needles

The iron needles could be cut from old bicycle spokes. Each needle measures 1 inch (25 mm) long. One end is sharpened to a point and the other end is filed according to need. The needles should be polished.

There are three kinds of needles: (1) A drawing needle has a point like a ball-point pen and can be used to draw lines. (2) A scorching needle has a thicker point filed into a slanting tip with a cross-section of a horseshoe. It is used for scorching certain spots or strips. (3) A knifelike needle with a blade that's thin and flat is used to draw even lines like ripples, willow twigs, or horse tails.

All three kinds of needles come in three different sizes: big, medium, and small. Another flat-top needle is used to dot mosses. Other tools include a candle, a pair of tweezers, a small wooden board, and a bowl of water.

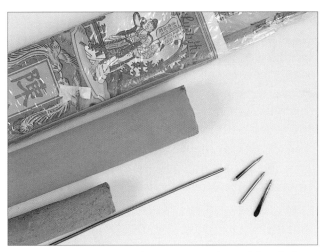

Chinese joss stick and bicycle spoke tips make useful tools for gourd pyrography.

Creating a Joss Stick and Needle Tool

Insert the point of the needle into the center of one end of the joss stick about ⅜ inch (1 cm) deep. Then light the joss stick with the candle and push the needle slowly into the stick by pressing it on the wooden board until the other end of the needle has about ¼ inch (6 mm) exposed like a pencil lead. The needle is then ready to be used. The joss stick will crack if you press too hurriedly.

If you want to change the needle, just use a pair of tweezers to pull it out, drop it into the water bowl, and insert another one. The temperature of the needle can be adjusted. More force with the needle and a higher temperature is needed to draw the outlines. Use a complete stick with a heated needle. When rendering a spot or a strip, apply pressure evenly with a low-temperature needle. For low temperature, tear off one-third or one-half of the burning end and apply the needle slowly. Frequently press the needle tip with the wooden board so that not too long a needle head will be exposed.

Heat-Engraving Process

First use a pencil to draw a picture on the gourd; then use a hot drawing needle to trace the pencil outline and the main lines. Use the engraving needle to scorch out sunny and shaded sides. Of course, much depends on how deftly you can handle the needle pen to achieve a desired portrayal of the scene or an artful execution of the design.

For instance, by controlling the movement of one's fingers and wrist, either forcefully or lightly, you can produce a variety of lines, either thin or thick, deep or light, fluent or abrupt, to form an interesting and meaningful picture. It's similar to painting with a brush. Whether you apply the needle straight or slanted depends on what result you would like. There are no common rules.

Keep heat-engraved gourds in silk-lined boxes or wrap them up with silk to avoid exposure to strong sunlight. If exposed to sunlight, the color will turn dark while the design remains light and less distinct from the color of the gourd. Do not constantly rub or hold the engraved gourd in the hand; the engraving could fade or become mottled.

CHINESE GOURDS & TOOLS

Artist Wang Shixiang decorated these two pigeon-whistle gourds using big and small horseshoe-shaped heat-engraving pens. Wang says, "To copy a rubbing by heat engraving is not difficult. First draft the outline carefully with a pencil; then move your needle strictly on the outline. The nuance of the calligraphy will not be lost." (The original calligraphy was by Langting Xu.)

Artist Wang Shixiang calls this Tianjin pyroengraved cricket cage "Conferring a Duke's Title." On the pine is a beehive. Under it a young monkey cuddles near its mother to avoid being stung. The Chinese characters for bee (feng) and monkey (hou) are homophones for "to confer" and "duke," respectively. The effect is satirical.

This Tianjin molded gourd katydid or cricket cage, heat engraved by artist Wang Shixiang, depicts a Chinese landscape from the northern school of painting. The gourd was grown in a ceramic mold to shape it.

SOLID-TIP WOOD BURNER

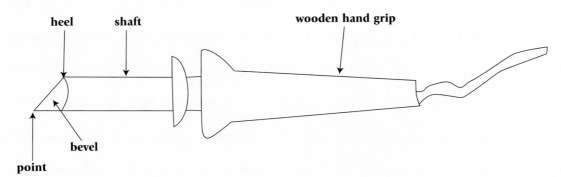

Here's the working end of a solid-tip wood burner.
Drawing by Duane Teeter

WOOD BURNERS AND TIPS

Many different kinds of wood burners and pyrography pens are available. Here's how the classic solid-tip wood burner looks. You need to choose one that best suits your style. In the chapter "Pyrographic Art," you'll discover the many different tools and techniques that over fifty pyrography artists use in their work.

In the chapter "Pyrographic Art," we'll look over the shoulder of three artists, Duane Teeter, Susan Sweet, and Carolyn Rushton, as they create several pyroengraved gourds using widely available pyrography tools: M. M. Newman's Hot Tool, Razertip Industries' SSD10 Razertip burner, and Leisure Time Products' Detail Master IV Sabre.

Two other companies which manufacture a separate, solid-state, temperature-controlled power supply are Colwood Electronics' Detailer and Nibsburner brand wood burner. Most companies manufacture either fixed-tip pens or pens with interchangeable tips. Heat is lost at every connection, so fixed-tip pens will have more heat at the working end than pens with interchangeable tips. All pyrography craft-tool companies manufacture power supplies which allow you to plug in two pens at one time, although only one pen will be hot at a time.

See the Pyrography Pens Chart (page 129) to discover the vast variety of burning pens available and choose an appropriate pen for your project.

Finding the Right Tip

Here are the most widely used wood-burning tip shapes that work with different wood-burning systems for gourds.

The Razertip #1M is used for cutting lines on burning systems.

The Razertip #5M is used for shading on burning systems.

The Razertip #9 is used for drawing on burning systems.

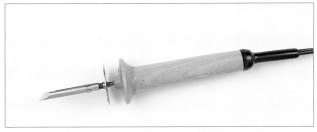

The Hot Tool with a standard tip is a solid tip wood burner.

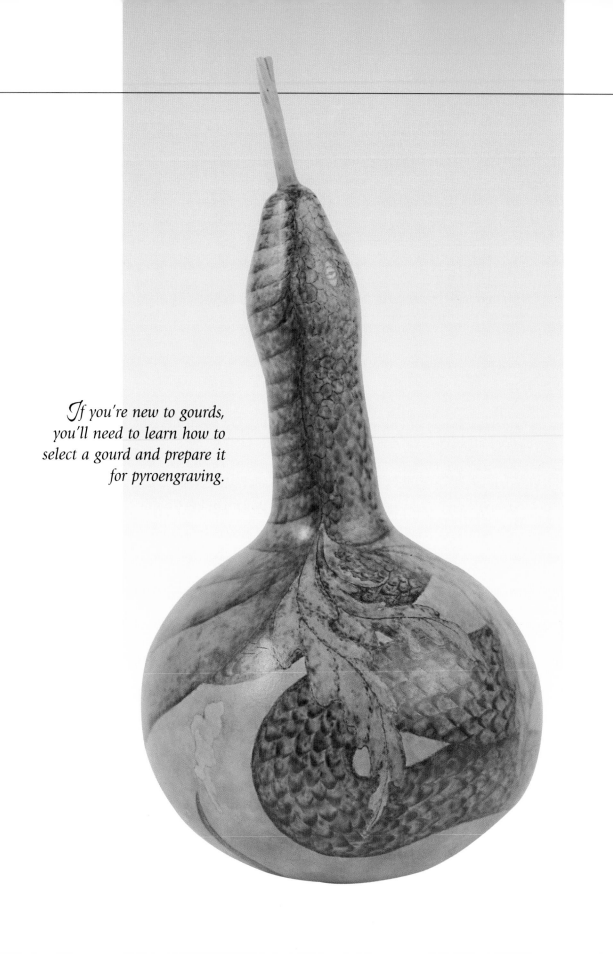

If you're new to gourds, you'll need to learn how to select a gourd and prepare it for pyroengraving.

GOURD PREP
& WORK BASICS

FIND THE BEST GOURD

If you're new to gourds, you'll need to learn how to choose an appropriate gourd and prepare it for pyroengraving. Gourd farms are found all over the United States, mostly in the middle and southern latitudes, as well as in Canada, Europe, Asia, and Down Under. Gourds grow wild and on farms in many parts of the African continent.

Of course, it's most fun to go into fields and pick your own gourds. If that isn't feasible, most growers offer a mail-order service. You can choose gourds that are shaped like basketballs, pears, figure eights (bottles), or gourds with straight or curved "handles." Some gourds will roll around and some will sit flat. As you read this book, you'll get a sampling of all the different shapes you can choose from.

Choose a gourd that has a reasonably thick shell. Avoid using a larger gourd with a shell less than ¼ inch (6 mm) thick. The thickness won't affect your burning, but after all that work, you don't want your gourd to crack easily if you happen to drop it.

Here are some of the various natural shapes of gourds, some with stems intact, pyroengraved by artist Duane Teeter.

After considering the shape and thickness, note the gourd's color. Most growers only sell "dirty" gourds; the moldy skin and sand from the field still cling to the gourd. Brush some dirt away so that you can see the color of the gourd underneath. Choose gourds that are as light in color as possible. With time, they'll darken naturally, and you'll want your burning to contrast with the gourd's natural color.

To ensure a very light-colored gourd, buy a mature green gourd. You'll know the gourd is mature if at least 6 inches (15 cm) of brown stem emerged from the gourd before it was cut. A reputable grower will not harvest a green gourd until it is mature. Using a regular butter knife (not serrated) or a bone awl, scrape the very thin epidermis off the gourd. The epidermal layer is one cell thick; don't cut into the gourd, just scrape. The skin scrapes off very easily. After the skin has been removed, wipe the gourd with a dilute bleach solution to retard any mold growth. Continue to wipe the gourd once a week with the mild bleach solution. The gourd will dry much faster after the green scraping and will dry with a very lightly colored, creamy skin.

SCRAPING THE GOURD

These green gourds are mature for harvesting, but they're not yet dried for craft work. They can have many different color patterns. Here they are before (left) and after (right) scraping.

 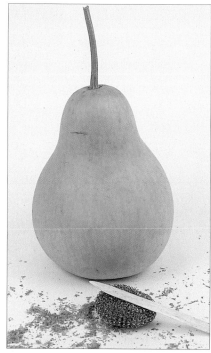

This green Martin house gourd (left) is being scraped clean of its epidermis with a bone awl. Here's the green Martin house gourd (right) scraped clean.

CLEAN & REMOVE THE GOURD'S SKIN

When you first acquire your dried gourd, it will probably have a dry, black, moldy skin still attached to its surface. Be thankful. The mold has actually made the job easier because it has loosened the skin.

Prepare the gourd for scrubbing in one of these three ways: (1) Put the gourd out in the rain for a few hours. (2) Put the gourd into a black plastic bag with about 2 cups of water. Tightly seal the bag and place it in the sun for a couple of hours. (3) Immerse the gourd in a tub of water for a couple of hours with a thick wet towel on top of it to fully wet the skin.

Turn the gourds periodically to keep them wet. After the gourd has been through the water treat-ment, use a stainless-steel scour-ing pad to wipe off all the mold and bits of outer skin still sticking to it. Then rinse and let dry. Your gourd is now ready for crafting! Don't rush the water treatment. It really does make the scouring job very easy. If you rush the treat-ment, you'll pay later with elbow grease.

This dried, moldy gourd is fresh from the field.

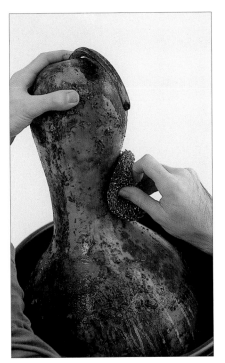
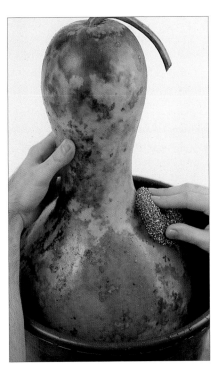

Prepare to scrub the moldy skin from the gourd. Soak the gourd in water for several hours; then use a stainless steel pot scrubber. Very shortly the scoured gourd will be ready for rinsing.

SKETCH THE DESIGN

Begin drawing the design. It's easier to visualize a design for a lidded container with the gourd in one piece. Sketch your design with a soft pencil, working the cut line for the lid into the design. Don't forget to take into account the weight of the lid after it will be cut off. You don't want a top-heavy lid. After burning, cut off the top and clean the inside of the gourd.

Defects, Warts & Blemishes

Natural imperfections in the skin of the gourd, such as little warts or bruises from growing or insects, can help inspire design ideas. You can often easily incorporate them into your burning.

CLEAN INSIDE THE GOURD

Cut the gourd open with an X-acto knife with #15 or the #27 saw blades. Or use a miniature hand-held jigsaw to make the cuts. For a lidded piece, make the cuts very carefully so that they will fit back together without gapping. Do NOT sand the cut line if this is a lidded piece.

For cleaning out the gourd guts, papery fiber, and seeds, use a sharpened serving spoon or one of the various sets of gourd scrapers on the market.

Here's another cleaning method: Fill the gourd with water and let it sit for a couple of days. Then pour out the water, add fresh water and

HIDING DEFECTS

The defect in this gourd becomes the center of the magnolia-flower design by Gretchen Ceteras.

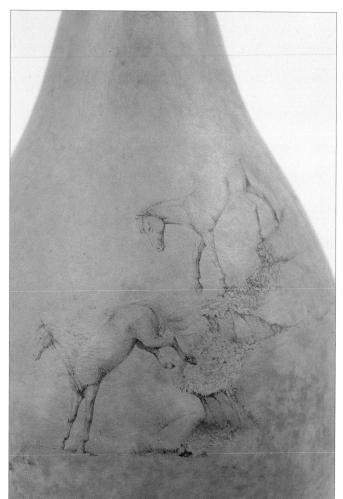

Artist Betty Finch, taking advantage of the defects in this gourd, made bluffs in a hillside down which horses walk.

some gravel, and shake the gourd vigorously. Pour out the water and gravel and let the gourd dry. This process will produce a clean gourd; however, the water in the gourd can darken the shell somewhat, making some pyrography more difficult to distinguish.

After cleaning and scraping the inside of the shell, use rough sandpaper and a stainless-steel scouring pad to go over it again. When the inside of the gourd seems smooth enough, you're done.

HOW ONE ARTIST GETS TO WORK

To prepare a gourd for wood burning, pyrography artist Betty Finch washes it with a pot scrubber. She scrapes any stubborn areas with a pocket knife and scrubs it again with the pot scrubber. Any tiny bits of skin left on the gourd will cause dark flared spots as she work because the skin burns at a lower temperature than the shell.

Green, scraped gourds are ideal for pyroengraving. Details of engraving will show up well against the stain-free light, even-colored surface of a green gourd that has been scraped clean. Choose a gourd late in the growing season that has a dry stem and a relatively blemish-free living skin. Then set to work with your bone awl or butter knife. Use a knife to scrape stubborn areas around the blossom scar, stem, and blemishes. After scraping,

Respirator or particle dust mask.

place the gourd in a well-ventilated sunny window to dry. The gourd may seep moisture that will cause a stain if it is not turned frequently. Green gourds that have been scraped will dry quickly and can be ready to use when all moisture escapes. Seeds inside the gourd may not rattle when the gourd is dry. To check for dampness, Finch advises holding the gourd to your cheek; if part of the gourd feels cool, it isn't ready.

It's important to plan your design before you begin burning. You cannot "erase" mistakes. Decide which side of the gourd you want to use as a focal point. Place the gourd on a flat surface

and note which side leans away. Use the side that offers the best view—the best canvas—with the least distortion due to curves.

You don't need to reject misshapen or blemished gourds. In your pyroengraving, these blemishes can be incorporated into your work to enhance the uniqueness and to add value to the finished piece.

Decide what height you'll want to view the gourd from. Do you plan to have it sit on a low coffee table or on a high fireplace mantel? Decide what the horizon line will be when you place your subject. With a pencil, lightly block out the design on the gourd. First sketch the subject in a size and shape that fits within the desired area, keeping realistic objects in proportion. Look at the gourd to check the position of your subject. If it will be viewed while you are sitting, you'll want to sit to look at your pencil sketch on the gourd. Wipe away any unwanted marks with a damp cloth.

Use very slow pen movements to burn in the darkest areas first. These darkest spots will be the safest areas to experiment with how fast you'll need to move your hand to create the desired color. Begin work with a low temperature and gradually increase it until slow movement produces a dark line that doesn't scorch the surface of the gourd. Many artists control darkness with the speed of hand movements rather than with low, medium, or high temperature settings.

Now burn in the general outline of the sketch and remove the pencil marks with a damp rag. Be sure to allow the gourd to dry completely after wiping it with a damp rag before you continue to burn in your design. Any dampness will throw off your feeling for hand movement speed because the dampness will slow the burning. Remove the pencil sketch before you add burned-in details. Otherwise, pencil marks may be sealed under a clear coat formed by heated resins within the gourd. Once they have been sealed, you won't be able to remove these pencil marks except by sanding.

As you work, clean the tip of your pyrography pen periodically. A stainless-steel scouring pad works well for cleaning the tip. Of course, you'll want to turn off the wood burner before cleaning the tip. Be careful if you use steel wool; it can be set on fire, especially when it contains wood particles.

Add the desired half-tones (areas neither dark or light but in between), using faster hand movements. To fill in lighter areas, you'll want to use rapid repetitive movements. Follow the image's contours to create the desired three-dimensional effect. Be aware that light shading will fade considerably within a few months.

BURNING YOUR DESIGN: SAFETY TIPS & HELPFUL HINTS

Here are helpful hints and important safety tips for a successful project.

1 Hold the burner the same way you hold a pencil.

2 Hold the pen so that the heat goes up, not back into the pen.

3 When making curved lines, use your little finger as a support and rotate your hand around your little finger.

4 Turn the work instead of your hand whenever possible. That way your hand is always in the same, comfortable, controlled position.

5 Rapid drawing with the pen will leave a lighter line than slow drawing with the pen.

6 Shade away from your hard lines.

7 Let the heat do the work. Do not bear down with the pen. If you're not getting the burn you want, turn up the heat a half notch or slow down. Pushing harder with the pen will only damage the pen and possibly cause it to slip and damage your work or your hand.

8 Don't inhale the smoke. A fan placed in front of the work area, pulling the air away from you, will pull the smoke away from you as well. However, the draft can also serve to cool your pen and might affect the consistency of the burn. Experiment with the fan speed and placement so that you retain a consistent burn.

9 Keep the tips of your pens clean. As soon as you start burning, carbon begins to build up on the tip of the pen. Carbon is a wonderful insulator. Insulation keeps heat from being transferred. You want all the heat to be at the working end of your pen, so frequently wipe off the carbon buildup. A stainless-steel scouring pad works very well with the soldering-iron type of burners. Manufacturers of solid-state burners each have their own cleaning systems, which you should use.

10 Do not change tips when the pen is hot. Heat causes metal to expand. If you have a pen with threaded tips, the threads will bond together when hot. Trying to remove them when they're hot will risk damaging the pen's heat element.

11 Even when the tool is cool enough to replace a tip, the tip you are removing is probably still hotter than your skin is capable of handling. Always use pliers or

SAFETY CHECKLIST

heavy-duty cord • gloves • mask • goggles • first-aid kit • ice some other appropriate tool to remove the tip and place the tip in a bowl where it will not burn your work surface or someone's curious fingers.

12 Take care of your pens even when you're not using them. Store them so that the tips are protected, preferably in the containers in which they were originally packaged.

13 Determine the right temperature for the line you are trying to make; then turn down the temperature a bit or speed up your movement slightly. You can always go over the line again to darken it. Work from light to dark. You don't want all your lines to be of the same intensity.

14 When you leave your work area, turn off the burning system. If your power supply does not have a light to indicate when it is on, keep your system plugged into a power strip with an ON/OFF light. When you leave the work area, turn off the power strip. The absence of the light on the strip will remind you that the power is off.

15 Always plug your power strip or power supply into the electrical outlet in the wall of your studio. If you must use an extension cord, use an extension cord that is marked heavy duty. Household extension cords (for lamps, radios, and clocks) are not rated for

---

FIRST AID FOR BURNS

If you get a burn, turn off your pyrography tool. Cool your skin as quickly as possible..

---

the wattage that you are using and will not supply the proper current to your power strip and power supply. They will also get too hot and become a fire hazard.

16 Keep your burning work area away from flammable fluids, curtains, and other combustible materials.

CLEANING HOT TIPS

It's important to keep the tip of the pyroengraving tool free from the carbon buildup which naturally occurs from the burning process. The carbon acts as an insulator and will reduce the amount of heat that reaches the gourd.

To clean the Hot Tool tip, artist Rimona Gale advises using a stainless-steel scouring pad. The scouring pad has lots of air pockets, which can act as an insulator for your fingers.

Hold the pad on one side and form it into a half ball. Just remember that metal is a good conductor. Carefully stab the Hot Tool tip into the center of the scouring pad with your right hand. With the left hand holding the scouring pad, grip the tip of the tool so that the tip is withdrawn from the pad. The friction from the pad will wipe off the carbon buildup.

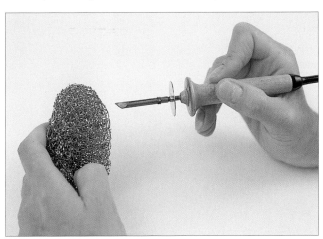 

Cleaning the Hot Tool tip.

Each artist uses pyrographic pens and tools to create distinct works of art.

PYROGRAPHIC ART

Learning the Craft

$\mathcal{H}$ere artists Duane Teeter, Carolyn Rushton, Susan Sweet, and Leah Comerford will walk you through a few projects step-by-step in the creation of their elegantly decorated gourds. Later in this chapter, you'll learn the secrets of the craft from over fifty accomplished pyrography artists. Be sure you also read the chapter "Gourd Prep & Work Basics."

In these projects, we'll identify the pen and manufacturer used in each step. Please refer to the Pyrography Pens Chart (page 129) to compare similar pens and tips from Razertip, Leisure Time, Nibsburner, and Colwood Electronics.

PEAR-SHAPED SAMPLER

ARTIST DUANE TEETER

BURNING TOOL
Hot Tool, standard tip

To understand various basic techniques, we'll show you step by step how Duane Teeter created this elegant pear-shaped gourd with its butterflies, floral designs, and geometric patterns. You can use these techniques when creating designs for your own projects.

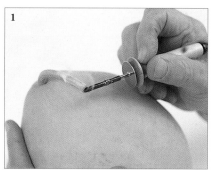

Before you begin work, seal the stem tip to prevent it from stripping or frizzing. Use the flat side of the standard tip of the Hot Tool to burn the cut edge of the stem.

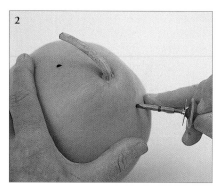

To create an arrow-point pattern, push the Hot Tool tip bevel side up into the gourd. Then rock the tip up to lengthen the arrow pattern you've created.

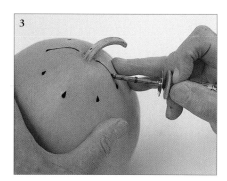

Beginning in the arrow point, use the bevel side down with the blade flat against the gourd and draw a line to the stem. Continue drawing the line down to the opposite arrow point.

With curving lines, connect the sides of two adjacent arrowheads. Use your little finger to stabilize the gourd and as a focus for the curve.

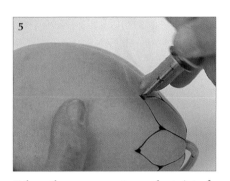

Where the curves meet, use the point of the tip to make another V-shaped dot. If you decide to add dye or paint to the gourd later, these burned-in dots make staining or painting easier because you won't have to paint in the sharp points.

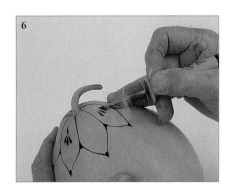

To create little teardrops, rock the burner from heel to toe with the blade fully touching the gourd.

Make another row of leaves, using the blade flat against the gourd.

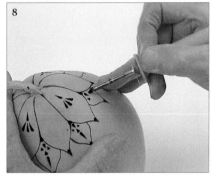

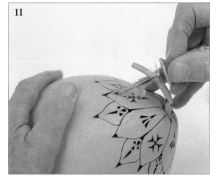

Make a series of dots with their points alternating up and down. To do this you'll turn the gourd back and forth while pushing the tip into the gourd.

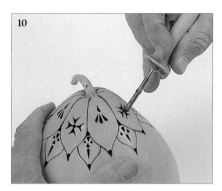

This design was made by turning the gourd and making shallow teardrops. Make the dot in the center by pushing the burner tip into the center of the pattern and rotating the burner.

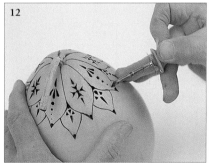

Make an elongated teardrop by pushing the burner blade flat against the gourd, away from you and lifting the tip up away from the gourd.

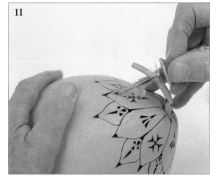

Make a series of smaller and smaller circles by adjusting the depth to which you push the burner tip into the gourd. With the last circle, the tip barely touches the gourd.

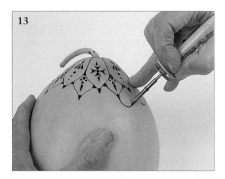

Beginning at the tip of the last row of leaves, make a curved line which begins to spiral back toward itself. Make a mirror image spiral, starting from the next leaf tip from the previous row.

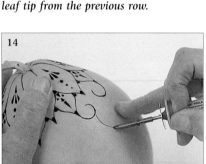

Bring the curved line down from the two spirals.

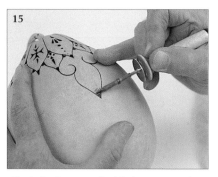

Shade by keeping the blade against the gourd. If the point is perpendicular to the surface, the tip will jump around.

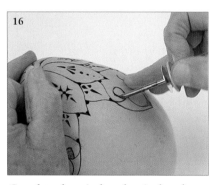

Complete the spiral so that it sharply curves back on itself.

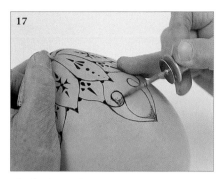

Shade the curl.

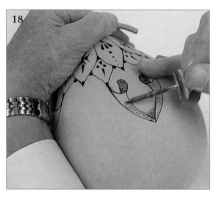

Shade by making a winding mountain road. The lines wind around and do not touch each other.

Detail of the shaded area.

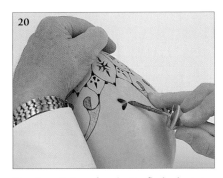

Create a flat surface butterfly by laying the burner blade down sideways against the surface. Turn the gourd for each butterfly wing.

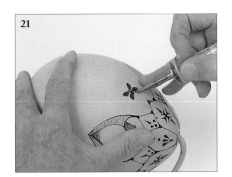

Lightly draw in the butterfly's body and antennae.

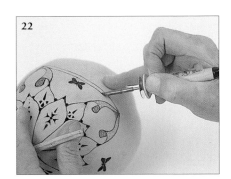

Draw a series of parallel lines.

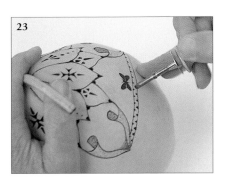

Make a zigzag line within the lines by alternating dots along one margin, then along another. Turn the gourd instead of turning the burner.

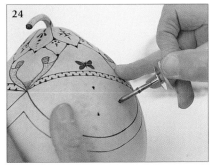

You can create most patterns by using four dots as compass points.

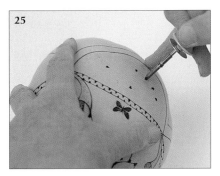

This will be an oval pattern, so add more dots between the original four to create an oval.

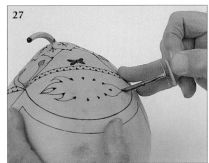

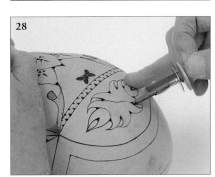

Begin to connect the tips of the dots with curved lines. It can get tricky deciding which dots to connect. Try to visualize what you want to happen.

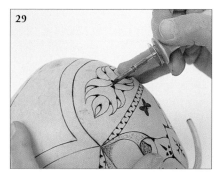

Add ornamentation with a couple of elongated teardrops.

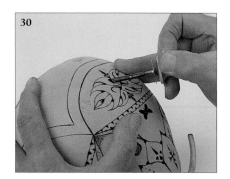

Here's a very elongated teardrop. You can see a finished teardrop directly below the burner tip.

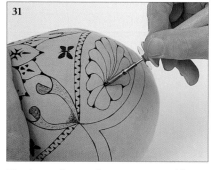

Here's another oval pattern created by connecting dots. In the center of the flower is a circular dot.

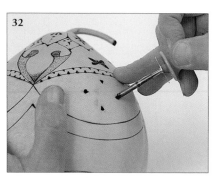

These dots are arranged in a more conventional compass pattern.

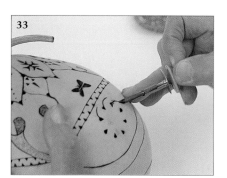

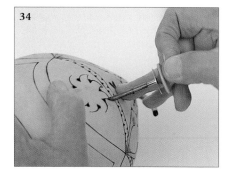

A curved line is brought out from each dot's tip. Then lines are connected to the adjacent dot.

Artist Robin McBride Scott draws lines, holding the tip so that its small pointed end is the only part of the tip touching the gourd. For shading, she turns the tip so that the flat surface of the pointed end lies on the gourd.

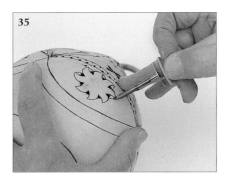

Dimension is added.

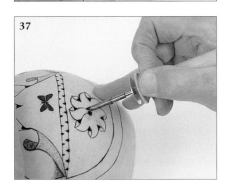

Place a small circular dot in the center and bring petals to the center.

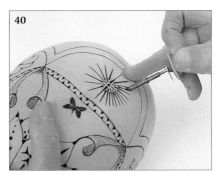

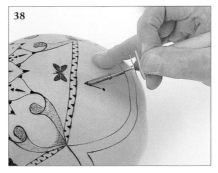

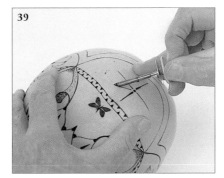

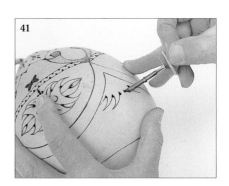

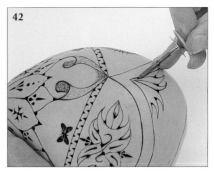

This pattern is created from many lines of differing lengths that radiate from a center dot.

Connect an arc of dots. Then connect the dots to the vertex.

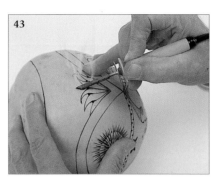

An elongated teardrop is being burned below the middle of the design.

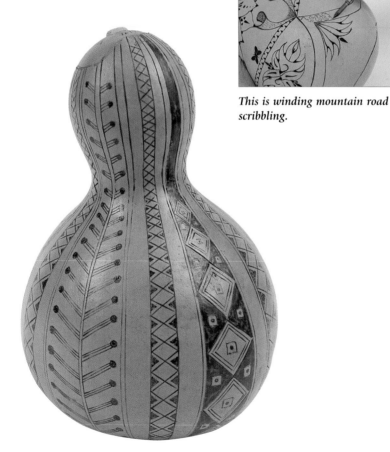

This is winding mountain road scribbling.

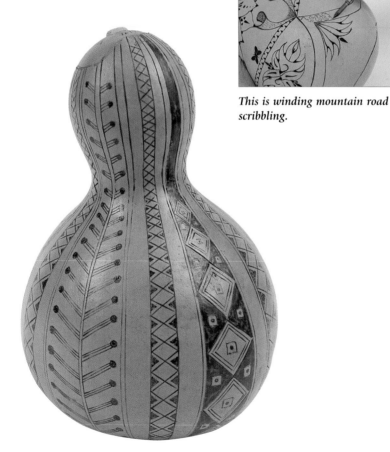

Geometric Design by artist Gretchen Ceteras.

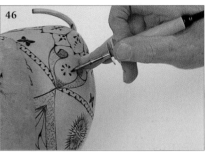

Four small teardrops, with teardrops carefully centered in between them, and teardrops between those, eventually build into a flower with many petals.

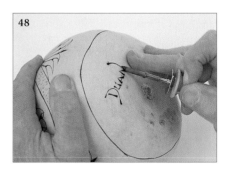

The artist Duane Teeter signs his work with the same standard tip he has used throughout his pyrography work.

TALL SAMPLER

**ARTIST
DUANE TEETER**

**BURNING
TOOL**
Hot Tool,
standard tip

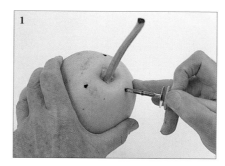

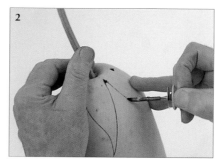

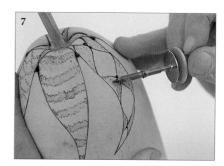

Singe the stem. Divide the elongated gourd into thirds with three dots burned into the top of the gourd. Then introduce three more dots between the original three to divide the gourd into six parts. Connect adjacent dots with long, curving petals. To burn the lines, use the full blade of the burner, not just the tip. Connect the dots to the stem with a six-pointed star.

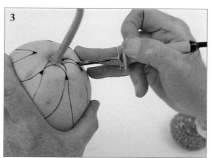

This is scribble shading.

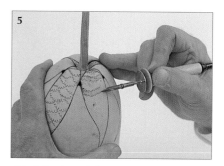

This is back and forth shading.

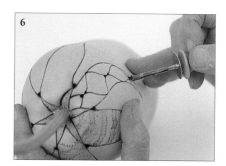

The artist draws a pattern on the petal.

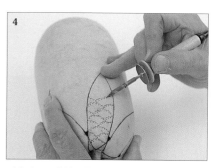

Here is tiny scribbling.

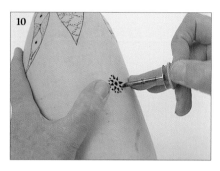

Tiny dots give depth to these butterfly dots.

You can add elongated teardrops, dots, and other patterns to build the design.

Arrange the elongated dots in a circle. Make a circular dot in the middle by putting the burner straight down into the gourd and turning the burner.

Add lines to extend a design.

Web Container with lid by artist Carol Morrison

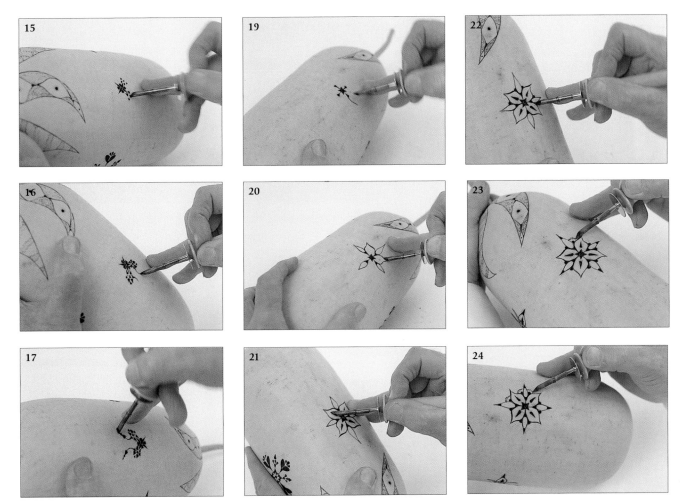

Build out the pattern.

You can create the four-sided figure in the middle by burning four dots with the points facing out and the sides touching. Burn the outer row of elongated dots with points facing inward and touching the first figure. Build the pattern out, little by little.

MORE WAYS TO BUILD A VARIETY OF PATTERNS

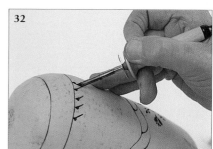

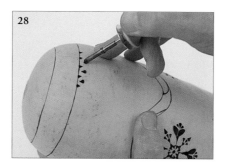

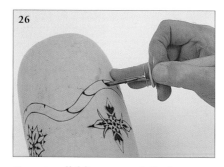

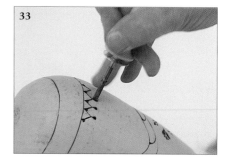

Burn parallel lines around the lower part of the gourd. Connect the parallel lines to make a barber-pole spiral.

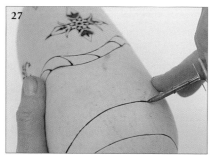

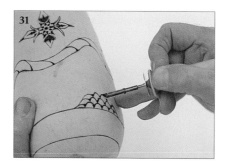

Burn five dots with tips facing up. Then burn four dots with tips facing down between the first five dots. Build the pattern out.

Build the pyramid pattern with dots and extended lines.

Burn two parallel lines around the base of the gourd.

Make another pattern of five and four dots, but connect them this time with curved lines to form hillocks.

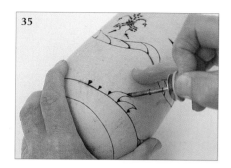

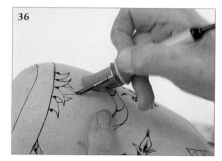

Here are a few ways to connect the dots, creating patterns resembling leaves or flames.

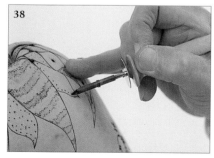

Add more long curving petals between existing petals. Create shading.

Here are two more views of the completed tall sampler gourd.

OWL EYES

ARTIST DUANE TEETER

BURNING TOOL
Hot Tool, standard tip

With lines, shading, and pyramid dots to create feathers, the standing owl is complete.

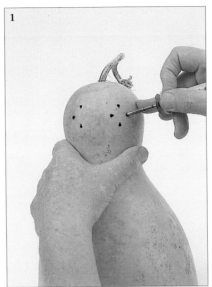

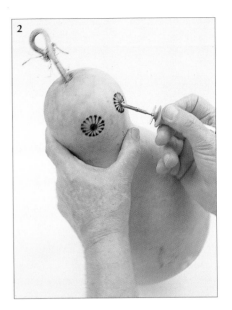

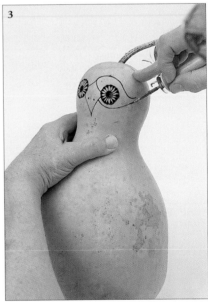

Burn four dots with the tips facing toward the center of the circle formed by dots. Then fill in the space between the dots with three more evenly burned dots. Burn a circle for the owl's pupil by pushing the burner point straight into the gourd and turning to make an even, black circle. Burn the lines defining the nose and eyes.

FROG

ARTIST SUSAN SWEET

BURNING TOOLS
Hot Tool, standard tip; Razertip, #1S, #5M, #5S, #9S tips

Removing the Top

Sketch the cut line with a pencil. Insert an X-acto knife blade into the gourd at the cut line to make a slot for the saw blade. You'll make the actual cut with an X-acto #15 or #27 saw blade, or you can use a mini-jigsaw to cut the top off the gourd. We used a Minicraft jigsaw.

Use pencil, X-acto, and mini-jigsaw.

Clean the Gourd

Scrape out the gourd guts, noting safety precautions and wearing a particle dust mask. Use coarse sandpaper to smooth the opening. A stainless-steel scouring pad can help scrape out and smooth the inside of the gourd. Use a sanding wheel on a high-speed grinder or drill to round the lip of the gourd. We've used a Minicraft drill.

SAFETY NOTE

Many people are highly allergic to gourd guts. Be sure to wear a dust mask when cleaning inside the gourd. You may also dampen the gourd's insides to keep the dust from becoming airborne.

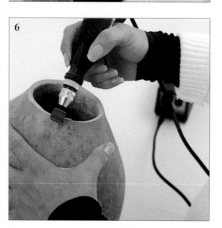

Scrape, use sandpaper, drill.

Draw the Pattern

Scribe a circle with a pair of dividers or with a compass. Complete the pencil drawing of the pattern you want to burn into the gourd.

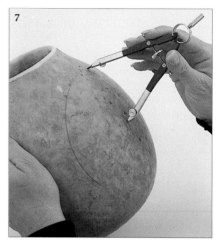

Concentric circles are first drawn with a pencil and burned in with a Hot Tool.

Use the Hot Tool to burn the two concentric circles outside the design. Keep the blade of the Hot Tool flat against the surface. Burn with the whole blade, not just the tip.

Outline the frog design with the Razertip #1S pen. A wet sponge will erase the pencil lines.

Shade and Stipple

Shade the throat with the Razertip #5S pen. Lots of tiny dots will create a stipple effect. Shade the frog's belly with the Razertip #9S pen for a more open stipple effect. You can

fill the area in later with finer stippling, if you wish. Shade leaves with the Razertip #5M pen by drawing thin lines to represent the longitudinal veins. Use a Razertip #9S for finer stippling on the belly.

After burning in the design, erase the pencil lines, otherwise they'll show.

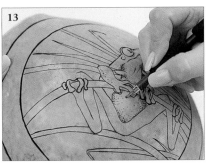

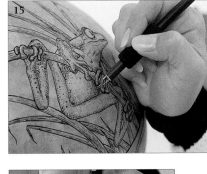

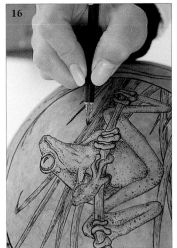

Note how stippling, shading, and striation add depth and interest to the figures.

Then use the Razertip #5M for more leaf veins, and the Razertip #1S to outline the salamander outer motif.

Here's the finished pyroengraved frog gourd with salamanders crawling round.

Paint the Gourd

To paint the gourd, use a fine brush and acrylic paint and brush away from the burned lines. Use a soft cotton cloth to remove unwanted paint. You can also remove paint with a dry, short-bristle brush that absorbs paint. A moistened, soft cloth removes the last of the paint. Reddish leather dye is painted around the salamander.

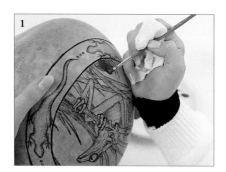

Here's the process of painting and removing paint.

FRIENDLY ADVICE

ARTIST LEAH COMERFORD

BURNING TOOL
Hot Tool, needle tip

Leah Comerford uses the Hot Tool with the needle tip for all her work.

Here's Comerford's description of her work process: "After drawing the scene in pencil, I use the Hot Tool with the needle tip to lightly follow every line. I hold the tool like a sketching pencil and try not to make any solid lines with this first burning. Holding the tool very close to the gourd surface, perpendicular to the line, and barely touching the first ⅛ inch (3 mm) of the tip to the gourd (just enough to cause a light burn), I begin to skim over the penciled lines. The natural unevenness of the gourd surface creates a stippled look to the burned outlines.

"If I'm certain that an area will later require dark shading, or if an object needs a hard line, I make a solid, thin burn line. (The fish bowl was started with a solid line.) For this kind of line, I keep the tool going in the same direction as the penciled line, tilt the tip more toward the gourd so that little more than the end point meets the gourd, and then move the tip in slow, gentle increments along the line."

After she completes burn sketching, she chooses one area of the scene and begins shading. Using the same light touch, she adds more stippling to create shadows. For deep shadows, she advises that you apply more pressure on the tip while still creating a dotted pattern, not burned grooves. Then create stipples away from the deepest part of the shadow, leaving fewer and fewer burned dots until the shadow fades away.

Comerford explains: "As soon as one portion of the scene shows a variety of shading, I start working around the gourd until shadows have been applied everywhere. After the second round of burning, I choose part of the scene that needs more definition (a creature's hair, for instance), and I work in that area until I'm satisfied with the detailing. Now I have this newly detailed section to use as a guide. I work my way around the gourd a third time, filling in details as needed.

"During this phase, I occasionally hold the tool like a pen and point it straight down to burn in tiny details-usually around the eyes or mouths of the characters. Otherwise, I continue to hold the tool like a sketching pencil and stipple, layer upon layer, throughout the burning process. Toward the end, I use the side of the tip to burn grooves into any shadows that need to be nearly black in appearance."

For a medium-size gourd, fully burning a gourd scene this way can take 40 to 60 hours. Gentle burning is a very slow process. If you listen to music and relax into the slowness, "two hours goes by in a wink," Comerford says. Limit a burning session to 2 hours. Holding the tool lightly, while keeping it steady and close to the gourd surface, really strains finger muscles and nerves.

After burning, Leah Comerford uses watercolors to color the scene. Then she uses colored pencils and enhances highlights with minimal carving, using a diamond bit in a high-speed rotary tool.

FRIENDLY ADVICE

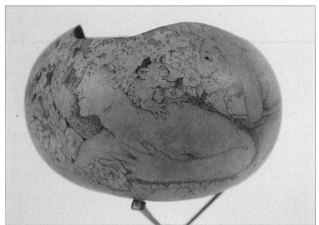

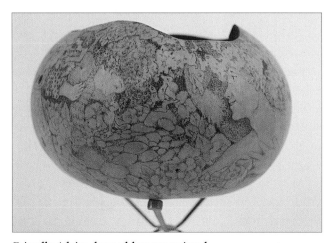

Friendly Advice, burned but not painted

Friendly Advice, painted

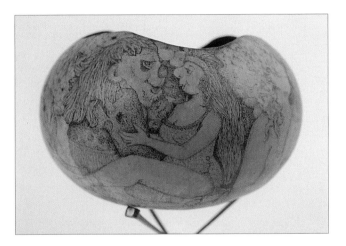

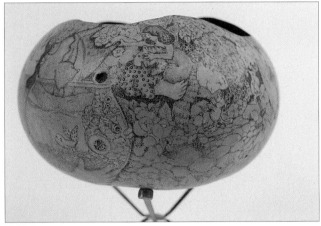

Friendly Advice, burned but not painted

Friendly Advice, painted

KISSING FIELDS

Add color little by little.

Leah Comerford uses acrylic paints to bring out the detail on this gourd.

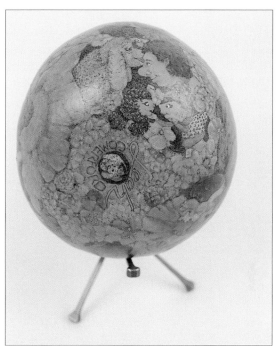

PONDEROSA (BUTTERFLY)

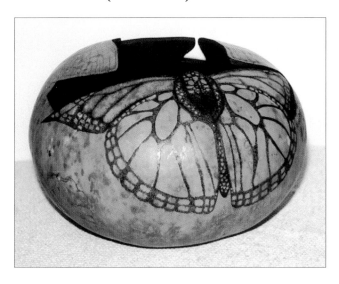

Here's Leah Comerford's Ponderosa, a butterfly bowl before and after adding color.
Jean and Les Ferber collection

TOTEMIC BIRD

ARTIST SUSAN SWEET

BURNING TOOL
Razertip, #1S, #5M, and #9S tips

Create triangular patterns, including the smaller ones on the wing, with the Razertip #5M pen. Use the Razertip #9S to draw little horseshoe shapes and stipple dots. The size of the dots depends on how much pressure you apply with the pen. For linear shading on the wings, use the Razertip #1S pen.

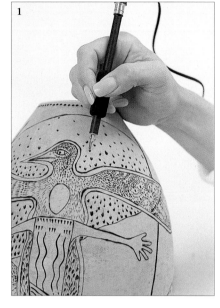

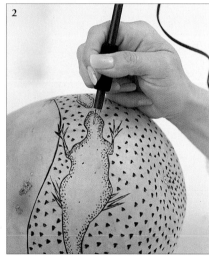

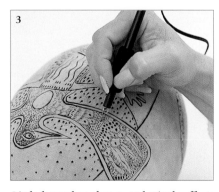

Little horseshoe shapes and stipple effects

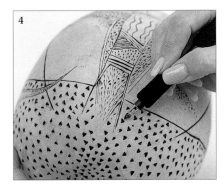

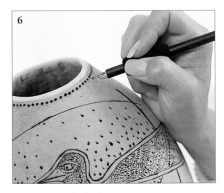

Triangular patterns

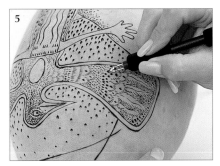

Dots around the lip

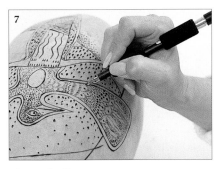

Linear shading

Underwater

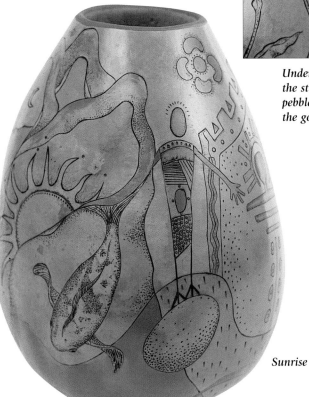

Underwater detail. Notice the stipple shading on the pebbles around the lip of the gourd.

Sunrise

HORSE'S HEAD

ARTIST CAROLYN RUSHTON

BURNING TOOL
Detail Master IV Sabre, #1A tip

Artist Carolyn Rushton begins a new project, like this horse's head with a pencil drawing. She carefully draws the design on the gourd, taking notice of the gourd's character and shape. Go over the pencil lines with a Detail Master #1A tip.

Use the full blade for drawing the outline. Turn the tip sideways to create shading and light, pencil-like strokes, such as those used on the horse's mane. Use just the tip of the pen to outline the eye and very lightly burn the eyeball to create a light tan color.

Shade the muzzle with short, quick strokes. The pen doesn't leave the surface while you're doing this; you'll be coloring as though you were using crayons. Finish with very light shading strokes with the pen.

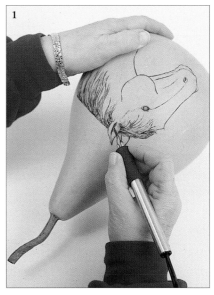

For ear hair, pull the #1A tip away from the center. The color will lighten as the tip is pulled away.

Horse's Head

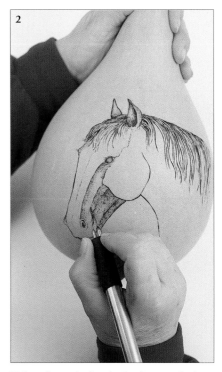

Using the #1A tip, shade the muzzle in short, quick strokes. The pen does not leave the surface. You're coloring as though you were using crayons.

FARM HOUSE

ARTIST CAROLYN RUSHTON

BURNING TOOL
Razertip, #1S tip

Use the Razertip #1S to outline pencil lines, create fine lines, and shade barn wood. You can shade the roof by laying the edge of the pen tip along one line and pulling away from the line. Also use the tip for the very fine lines of roof beams.

Using white paint, you can create snow on the barn.

Farm House

Fence with Sunflowers

Barn with Snow

MINI-BASKET GOURD

ARTIST CAROLYN RUSHTON

BURNING TOOL
Razertip, #1S, #1M, and
#HD1S-L tips

For this project use a thin-walled gourd. Draw the basket design with a pencil. Outline the pencil lines with a Razertip #1S. Make deeper burned lines at the top section. Then cut away the top sections of the gourd with an X-acto knife.

Spoon out the gourd guts with the edge of a sharpened spoon.

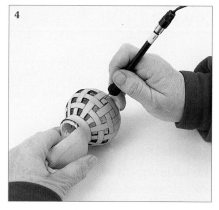

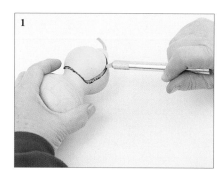

Draw the basket design, including the handle. Cut away the top section with an X-acto knife. Clean out the gourd guts with a sharpened spoon.

Burn in the basketweave pencil lines with a #1S pen.

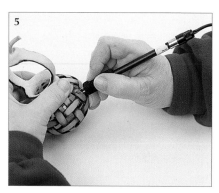

Cut out gourd sections with a Razertip #1M or #HD1S-L pen.

To shade for shadows, begin with the Razertip #1M pen blade against the line. Then gently slide the tip away from the line without leaving the surface. Extend the shading with individual vertical lines, making quick, short strokes.

After you sketch the vines and leaves on the handle with a pencil, use the #1S pen to outline the pencil lines.

Shade the vines and leaves with a #5S pen. Swivel the tip to make sharp curves more easily on the leaf lobes.

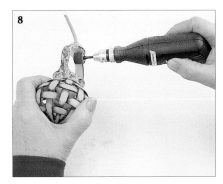

With a small triangular file, sharpen and smooth the corners in the weave. Use a sanding wheel on the Minicraft high-speed rotary tool to smooth the inside lip of the gourd and handle.

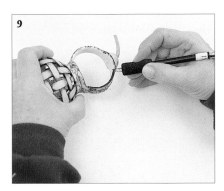

Finally, use the #1M pen to burn the cut edges of the gourd.

Cattail Bowl

Horse-Head Dipper

Cutout Oak-Leaf Basket

CARDINALS

ARTIST CAROLYN RUSHTON

BURNING TOOL
Hot Tool, transfer tip;
Detail Master IV
Sabre System, #1A tip

A Hot Tool with a transfer tip transfers the design to the gourd. A Detail Master IV Sabre draws in details. First, photocopy your design. Photocopiers and laser printers use a heat-fused ink. (If the paper comes out "hot," then heat-fused ink has been used. Make sure the laser printer or photocopier applies a generous amount of toner.) You'll want an image that has good contrast and black lines.

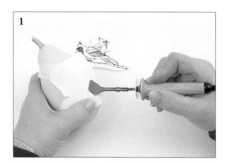

Put the photocopied design or image facedown against the gourd. Heat the back of the design with the Hot Tool transfer tip.

Carefully peel the paper from part of the gourd to make sure that the image has been transferred. If you find areas with no image transfer, lay the paper design back in its original place and again go over the area to be sure that the whole design transfers onto the gourd. You'll need to apply pressure with the transfer tip.

If you wish, you may transfer the design by using a piece of graphite paper between the paper design and the gourd. Trace the image with a sharp stylus. Do not use carbon paper.

Again go over the graphite image with a pencil to make the lines more visible.

After the design has been transferred, use the Detail Master #1A pen to burn over the pencil lines.

Use the Detail Master #1A pen to shade the cardinal's body and wings.

Cardinal Stencil Design

Tape the cardinal stencil into place.

Village Reflection, egg-shaped gourd

TROTTING HORSE

ARTIST BETTY FINCH

BURNING TOOL
Detail Master, #6A tip

Before you draw on the gourd, decide the size and shape of the area that the pattern will fill. A brown pencil works best, artist Betty Finch says. For this miniature Nigerian bottle gourd, I allowed the horses' extended legs to bend normally as the gourd is turned. If you rock the gourd back and forth, the front leg of the horse actually appears as though it were moving.

Determine size and shape of area pattern will fill. Brown pencil works best.

Burn in the darkest areas and lines.

Wash off pencil with a damp cloth.

Steer Cut from the Herd

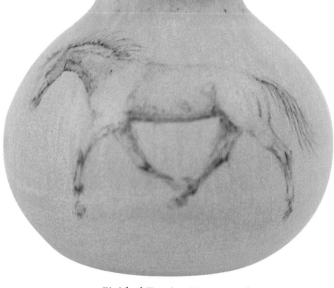

Finished Trotting Horse gourd

Mare and Foal

A Gourd Gallery with Artists' Secrets

ARTIST LIZA MUHLY

BURNING TOOL
Detail Master, #4A, #8B, and #8C tips; Hot Tool, standard tip

Artist Liza Muhly presses pyrography pen tips into the gourd to burn in her design. She prefers the Hot Tool with standard tip, used on its side, for lines and shading.

Courting Gourd Birds

ARTIST RHODA FORBES

BURNING TOOL
Colwood Detailer, #C and #S tips

For both the Lion and the Deer, artist Rhoda Forbes used the #C writing tip and the #S shading pen. She always works from light to dark to achieve her tonal values. She begins using the #C pen at a "4" heat setting, burning in the main features of the lion or deer and working back and forth with the tip. At the same heat setting, she begins creating the many layers of fine curved lines in the direction of growth of each hair. To produce the curve, she rolls the pen between her forefinger and thumb.

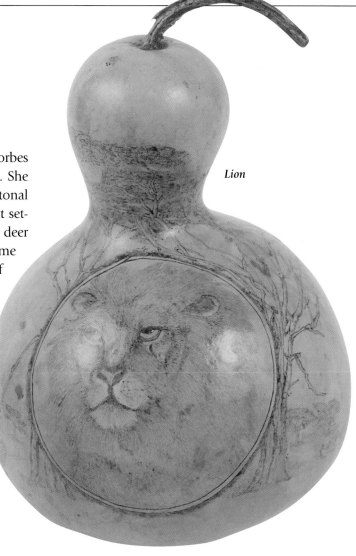

Lion

Deer

When she achieves the placement of hair, she sets the Colwood Detailer on the "5" heat setting and switches to the #S pen. When Forbes shades the animal, she pays special attention to the direction of light. Then she switches to the #C pen, still using the "5" heat setting, and adds a few curved strokes into the darker shaded areas to enhance individual hairs.

ARTIST DIC BONSETT

BURNING TOOL
Detail Master IV Sabre, #1C tip

Artist Dic Bonsett prefers smaller tips. These tips cut into the relatively soft gourd shell more easily because the ¼-inch pen rides more on the surface of the gourd and allows you to control the depth of the burn. Bonsett uses a homemade gourd chuck, from a universal adjustable clamp, for the pencil layout work. It also helps hold the gourd when he burns lots of repetitive, precise straight lines. For the rest of the work, he holds the gourd in his lap.

Round Pyramids

Classic Geometrics

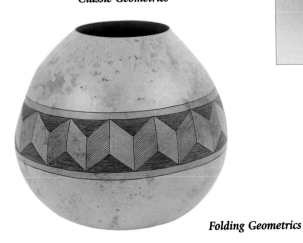

Folding Geometrics

Birds Walking

ARTIST CAROL MORRISON

BURNING TOOL
Hot Tool, standard tip

Carol Morrison creates elegant useful objects as well as gourd earrings. Find her earrings on page 124.

Business Card Holders

ARTIST MARK WHEELER

BURNING TOOL
Detail Master Excalibre model 8600, #6A
scribe, #2C, #1A tips

Wheeler prefers the #6A scribe pen for outlining, detail, and writing. The #2C works
well for shading and checkering, and the #1A
is useful for burning thin straight lines.
Wheeler says that he works with a cooler
temperature and then goes over lines several
times so that he does not overstate them with
too hot a tool. He does the same with shading, building from light to a darker color.

*Flowers and leaves on a pear-shaped
gourd with glass beads.*

Butterflies

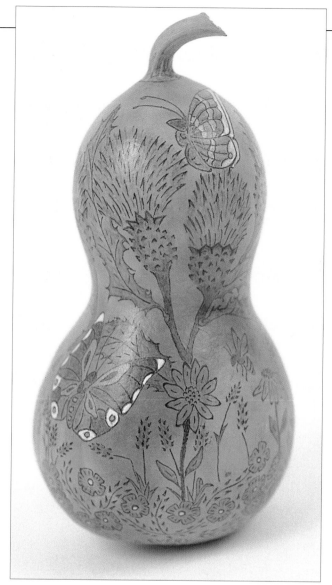

Thistles and Butterflies

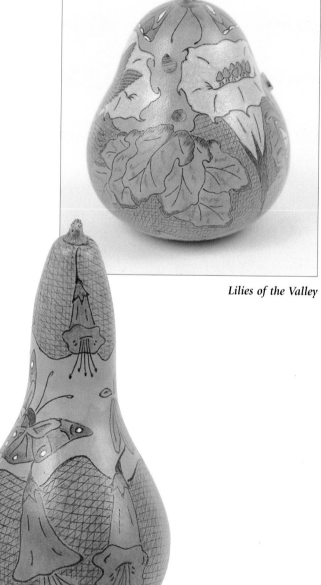

Lilies of the Valley

Lilies and Butterflies

ARTIST ANN MITCHELL

BURNING TOOL
Hot Tool, standard tip

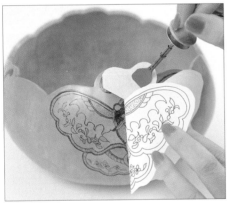

Artist Ann Mitchell uses a Hot Tool with a standard tip to transfer the photocopied design onto the gourd.

Chinese Butterfly gourd with a removable lid sitting on a stand.

ARTIST DON WEEKE

BURNING TOOL
Detail Master, #6B tip; Hot Tool, ³⁄₁₆-inch circle, ³⁄₈-inch circle, and standard tips; Detail Master, #1A pen

Don Weeke created a cuneiform design on the mask and jar with his #6B calligraphy pen. For the Spotted Continents jar he used the Hot Tool's ³⁄₁₆-inch circle, standard, and ³⁄₈-inch circle tips. He drew the Tri Pine design for the lidded gourd with strings with the

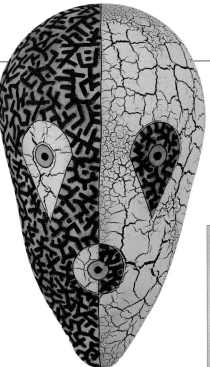

Cuneiform Mask

Spotted Continents

Cuneiform Jar

Tri-Pine with lid and decorative strings.

ARTIST ROBIN MCBRIDE SCOTT

BURNING TOOL
Walnut Hollow wood burner, spade tip

When she draws lines, Robin McBride Scott holds the tip so that its small pointed end is the only part of the tip touching the gourd. For shading, she turns the tip so that the flat surface of the pointed end lies on the gourd.

While burning for shading, Scott uses a small circular motion to make the shading smooth, and she doesn't burn into one area more than another. When shading in large areas, she uses the larger flat area of the tip and draws in a circular motion on the gourd. This causes the gourd surface to begin to change color.

For Celtic knot work, Scott uses the pointed end of the angled tip for line drawing. She holds the pen in her right hand with the pen resting on her ring finger

Eagle Spreading Wings. The blue spots are embedded bright beads.

Caribou

rather than a middle finger. "I usually pull the tip across on its side at about a 45-degree angle when I use it for drawing." When she creates deep lines in her knot work, she turns the heat up higher so that it burns into the gourd instead of simply shading the top surface.

"The key to getting smooth lines is always to draw or pull the tip away from you while keeping your hand braced against something and having the temperature setting just right on the wood burner. I usually have to adjust the temperature setting a little bit to be just right on every gourd. Each gourd is unique in its density and how much heat it takes to burn smoothly on it.

"When the heat is just right, the tip will glide across the gourd. If it is not hot enough, the tip will not recover quickly and will not keep burning evenly as you draw. If it's too hot, it will burn in deeply as you draw and may even discolor the surface surrounding where you were drawing your line," Scott says. If you practice drawing lines on gourd shards, you'll be able to feel how the tip glides across the gourd when the wood burner is set at the right temperature.

ARTIST NANCY RAVENHALL JOHNSON

BURNING TOOL
Colwood Electronics, pointed tip

Artist Nancy Ravenhall Johnson likes to be able to adjust the heat of her burning tool to suit the medium. "I don't like to have the heat up too high because the tip will often catch on the surface and scorch the piece. Using a pointed tip, I lay the first lines down very lightly. I work at one heat level all the way around the gourd. I darken my work one layer at a time. Thicker lines are made by going over the original lines, or laying another line directly next to an existing line to give the illusion of thickness or depth. For the fill, or areas that appear to be solid, I use a series of crosshatches or patterns."

Lucy (ducks)

ARTIST EMILY DILLARD

BURNING TOOL
Hot Tool, needle tip

Artist Emily Dillard cleaned and prepared a 47-inch bushel gourd. With a small hand-held jigsaw, she cut a jagged lid in the top. Then she sketched a jungle scene that covered the entire gourd, except the lid and bottom.

Using the Hot Tool with a needle tip, she wood-burned the sketch into the gourd. Later she burned a border around the lower rim of the lid to connect the scene when the lid was open. Then she added a few tree-top creatures.

"For color, I used colored pencils. I emphasized the wildlife by adding color to them, while leaving the background in the natural wood-burned tones. Then I decoupaged ferns and flowers onto the top and bottom of the gourd with Mod-Podge glue to give the viewer the impression of looking through foliage into the jungle," Dillard says. Using the same method, Dillard also created decoupage in the interior of the gourd and inside the lid.

Jungle

Emily Dillard has burned in the design, leaving the very top and bottom unmarked. She has begun adding color with colored pencils.

Ferns and flowers in a decoupage are added to the gourd's bottom and top.

Jungle details

ARTIST PAT WILKINSON

BURNING TOOL
Detail Master, #5A tip

Pat Wilkinson burns all her gourds with a single tip, the Detail Master, #5A.

Leap Frogs

Fox and Hare

Nursery

Sher Lynn Elliott-Widess collection

*Cut-out gourd
on pedestal*

Nursery
Sher Lynn Elliott-Widess collection

Children of the World

ARTIST SKIP HOWELL

BURNING TOOL
Hot Tool, ³⁄₁₆-inch circle tip

Petroglyphs

Iris

ARTIST SYLVIA WHITE

BURNING TOOL
Detail Master IV Sabre 100-watt, #1C, #5A, #6A, and #8A tips

For the inlaid gourd with black figures and spears, artist Sylvia White drew figures on paper and made several copies. She taped the copies to the gourd and traced them through the paper with her wood burner on low, using a #5A tip. This created a light line that White filled in with the #8A tip, as well as the #1C, which she used on its side.

For her Chinese gourd, she burned in the design using a #1C tip, then a small router to create the textured background.

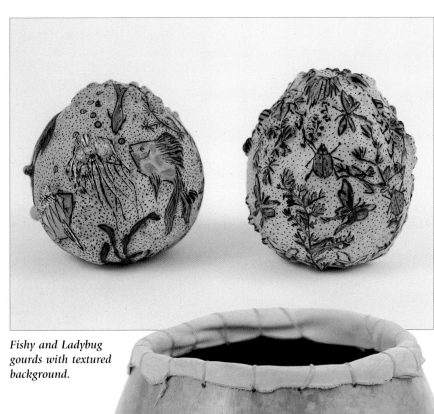

Fishy and Ladybug gourds with textured background.

Chinese Dragon

Inlay with Figures and Spears

ARTIST CAROL ST. PIERRE

BURNING TOOL
Hot Tool, standard and circle tips

The artist uses the standard tip for most of her work and occasionally uses the circle tip.

For the Swimming Turtle gourd, she cut out a lid in a turtle shape and decorated it to look like a turtle. Of course, this turtle-shaped lid fits neatly in place and also looks good sitting by itself.

Ferns Photo by George Post

Angel or Goddess
Photo by Anne Skeffington

Strawberry

Cats and People
Photo by Anne
Skeffington

Swimming Turtle Photo by Anne Skeffington

ARTIST NANCY MILLER

BURNING TOOL
Detail Master, #5A tip

The artist Nancy Miller used the Detail Master #5A pen to burn her design onto this Rose Triangle gourd. The shape and color of the finished work with its triple stem seem to suggest an unknown vegetable or fruit that's ripe and delicious.

Rose Triangle Photo by Hap Sakawa

ARTIST REBECCA BLACK

BURNING TOOL
Hot Tool with Dial-a-Temp, standard chisel and bent-needle tips

For outlining, artist Rebecca Black uses the standard chisel tip, and for fine line detail, she uses the bent-needle (stencil) tip. She uses the Dial-a-Temp 15-amp temperature control and turns the temperature up all the way for a darker brown color and turns the temperature down for lighter brown lines.

Tiger Family

ARTIST SHIRLEY BISBEE

BURNING TOOL
Colwood Olympiad #2009, #A rounded, #J custom, #S, #SQ, and #MC micro-writing tips

To create both curved and straight lines, artist Shirley Bisbee uses the wood-burning control unit with the #A rounded tip. The custom #J 90-degree angle tip is good for following concave surfaces and turning in a tight radius. For shading, use the #S tip and for flat burning and dark shading, use the #SQ tip. The #MC tip can be used for modeling, signing a name, or other writing.

Cat

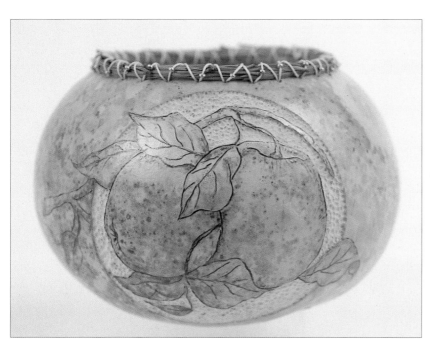

Apples

ARTIST ERNIE VELARDE

BURNING TOOL
1,000°F handmade tool

Ernie uses an inexpensive 1,000°F tool created by a friend, Joannis Mohrman. The only tip he uses is a shading spade that "I adapted and shaped myself to be more versatile." He draws with the edge of the spade tip.

Artist Ernie Velarde uses his handmade wood-burning tool.

Here's the shading spade.

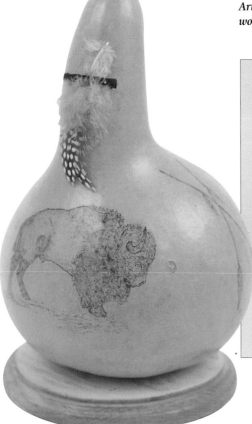

Bison

Bucking Bronco

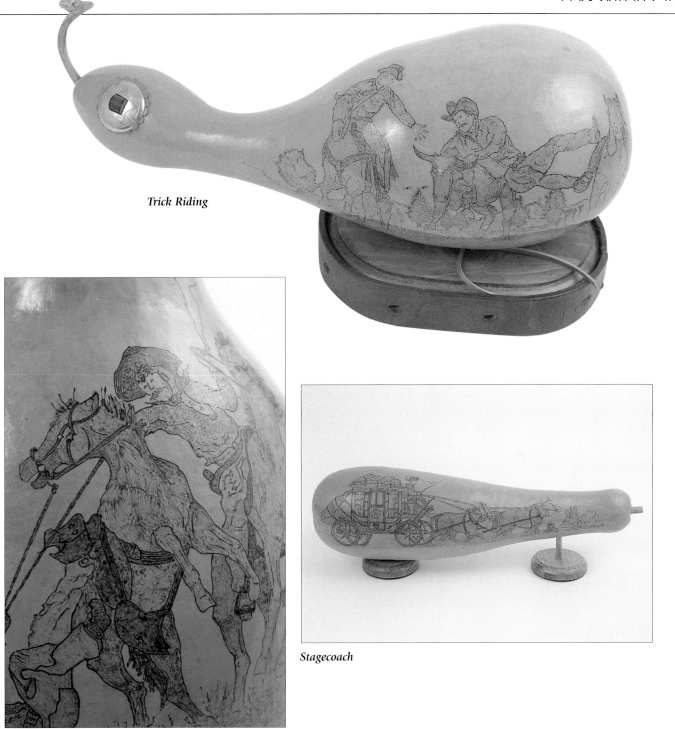

Trick Riding

Calf Wrestling

Stagecoach

ARTIST NICOLE DUPONT

BURNING TOOLS
Wall Lenk Professional Model, L30WBK, wedge tip, and WB25BT stencil tip; Colwood Super Pro II, shading S tip

First the artist Nicole DuPont drew the design onto the gourd with a soft pencil. Then she used the Wall Lenk wood burner with a wedge tip for the borders and edges of the pattern. She used the angled stencil tip for dot work on the mokihana berries.

For shading, she used the Colwood Super Pro II with a shading tip. She set the burner at a higher temperature for the darkest areas and used the rounded MC-45 degrees at a lower setting for the medium-dark areas. She kept the rounded tip constantly moving over the gourd, not letting the tip linger over one spot too long. This way, the area became gradually darker until it was the shade desired.

Maile and Mokihana Ipu

ARTIST TERESITA AMEZCUA

BURNING TOOL
Razertip, #1S, #7S, #9, #18S, and #18M tips

Teresita created this gourd with the Razertip pyroengraving tool. She used the #1S for outlining and the #9 and #18S for shading. For small circles, she used the #18S and for the hair on the field mice, she used the # 7S tip at a low temperature. The #18S and #18M were used for other detailing.

Climbing Flowers

ARTIST ROBERT LOGAN

BURNING TOOLS
Creative Wood Burner Jr. and Walnut Hollow Farm #4567, #5580, #5591 mini-universal, and #5592 flow-point, #5596 cone-point tips

First Robert pencils in the design. Then he uses the cone-point to outline the figures and design with the 950°F Creative Wood Burner Jr. pen. He then changes to the 750°F Walnut Hollow Farm pen, using the mini-universal point, to lightly burn in the ears, eyes, nose, mouth, and folds in skin and fur or hair. With the flow-point, he lightly burns in the fur. After each hair is lightly burned in, he goes over the areas again ,concentrating on folds and shaded areas.

Buffalo

To create the furry effect, he burns just enough; then he changes back to the cone point to lightly burnish the complete fur area, concentrating on folds and shaded areas. This gives the bears and buffalos a nice hairy look. He creates the grass with a flow-point tip and the trees, shrubs, and birds with the mini-universal point. He shades the mountains and hills with a cone-point tip, using it very lightly until he achieves the desired effect.

Bears

ARTIST KELLEE ANDERSON

BURNING TOOL
Craftsman 6-in-1 Creative Tool Kit, universal bit

Artist Kellee Anderson prefers using the standard size universal bit for her work, like this Panda.

ARTIST LINDA NOBLITT

BURNING TOOL
Detail Master, #5A and #7A tips

Linda Noblitt burns in her design with the Detail Master with #5A and #7A tips. She colored the wolf's fur with colored pencils. The paw prints were burnt in and shaded.

Wolf Container

Panda

ARTIST JOHN RIZZI

BURNING TOOL
Hot Tool, standard tip

John Rizzi uses a standard tip with his Hot Tool. On the lidded gourd Gold Bands, the artist applied gold leaf to the burned-in design. The Lizard gourd bears both gold and silver leaf.

He also decorates gourds with beads, threaded and tied inside the gourd.

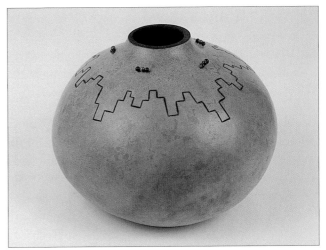

Beaded Gourd

Lizard

Gold Bands

ARTIST DENISE MYERS

BURNING TOOL
Detail Master, Excalibre model, #10B and ⅟16-inch fish-scale tips; Walnut Hollow, pointed tip

Denise Myers prefers the Detail Master #10B tip for almost everything she does. She says that the tip's configuration "makes it perfect for everything from creating the scaly skin around a bird's beak to the extremely fine hairs of an elk's face to the smooth hair of a tiger to the rough hair of a bear to the long, straight lines that divide the wildlife images from other areas of the gourd."

The temperature controls allow the artist to adjust the heat output of the pens. "I can create bone structure and musculature by carving an area lightly or repeatedly, to achieve the illusion of depth and texture." She also uses Walnut Hollow wood-burning pens for accent work. The pointed tips can burn holes or tiny circles into the works.

Finally, Myers adds color with acrylic paints to the finished pyrography.

Face of the Wolf, before and after color added.

The Power and the Glory, before and after color added.

ARTIST KATHY LEONARD

BURNING TOOL
Detail Master IV Sabre, #5A tip

Without using any patterns or preliminary sketches, Kathy Leonard burns in her design with her pyrography pen.

Roses

Hummingbirds

ARTIST BRENDA TRAFFIS

BURNING TOOL
Walnut Hollow, pointed tip

The artist draws the design with a tip shaped like a sharpened pencil. The flat sides of the tip fill in dark areas, and with the point Brenda Traffis draws lines and stipples in areas she wants shaded.

Basketweave Cannonball

ARTIST PAMELA HARMON

BURNING TOOL
Detail Master, #1A tip

The artist burned these designs with the #1A tip. She turns the tip on its side to shade large areas.

Note the stippled shading on this young girl design.

Young Girl

Lioness and Cub, two sides.

Blue Heron

ARTIST JANIS KOBE

BURNING TOOL
Detail Master, #5A tip

"I draw with the wood-burning tool in much the same way I would with a fine-line ink pen," says artist Janis Kobe. She sketches the initial drawing with a pencil directly on the gourd then uses pencil lines as a guide for wood burning.

Blue Heron, detail of nest.

ARTIST DIANE MERRILL

BURNING TOOL
Hot Tool, standard chisel tip

For all her artwork, Diane Merrill uses the Hot Tool with its standard chisel tip. She celebrates both primitive and modern. The gourd's shape, as with the Quail, may dictate its design. Her horses and bulls echo ancient artwork in the caves of France and Spain.

Ancient Horse Pitcher; influence from Altamira, Spain.

Acanthus Leaves

Quail Dr. Anna Webster collection

Horses lidded container; influence from Altamira, Spain.

Bull; influence from Lascaux, France.

Double Horses; influence from Niaux, France.

ARTIST KAY MIYAMOTO-MILL

BURNING TOOL
Detail Master, #1A and #5A tips

For these designs, artist Kay Miyamoto-Mill used the Detail Master wood-burning tool with the #1A tip to outline her design. She shaded various parts with the #5A tip.

Iris

Fuchsia

ARTIST SUSIE STINSON

BURNING TOOLS
Optima 1; Peter Child wood burner

For outline and shading, artist Susie Stinson uses the Optima 1. For really fine detail, she prefers the Peter Child wood burner.

Miniature Morning Glory pair

ARTIST JEAN MCCLINTOCK

BURNING TOOL
Dremel wood burner, chisel tip

The artist, Jean McClintock, uses the wood burner's chisel tip for her work.

Gourd Cricket Cages

ARTIST SUE WICKERSHAM

BURNING TOOLS
Detail Master III Dagger, #5A tip; Walnut Hollow Creative Wood Burner, universal tip

For sunflower petals and leaves, Sue Wickersham used the #5A pen. Inside the flower she used the universal tip. Note how the shape of the opening of the bowl assumes the outline of the flowers.

A leather thread stitched into the edge decorates the opening of the pinecone bowl.

Pinecone Bowl

Sunflower Bowl

ARTIST GLENDA MCBRIDE

BURNING TOOL
Dremel, grading and shading tips; Walnut Hollow wood burner, mini-flow technique tip

First Glenda McBride sands the gourd with 220-grit sandpaper to remove any rough spots. She traces pencil lines with a mini-flow technique point. While sketching and burning, the artist uses a thick piece of foam on her lap to support the gourd.

For shading, the artist holds the tool at an angle on the traced line and rolls the shading tool away from the line so that it goes from dark to light. McBride places the tool directly on the gourd to shade other areas. For a softer look, she holds the shading tool slightly above the gourd's surface.

Lighthouse detail

Lighthouse

Goose

ARTIST GARY DEVINE

BURNING TOOLS
Excalibre Plus wood burner; Colwood pen, #S ³⁄₁₆-inch shading and #H ³⁄₁₆-inch heavy-point tips

Gourd artist Gary Devine prefers to use the Excalibre Plus wood burner made by N. D. Robertson Enterprises in Ontario. It has a toggle that allows you to burn at a high or low setting.

You can also use a variety of pyrography pens, Devine says. Recently, he used the Colwood #S ³⁄₁₆-inch shading tip and the #H ³⁄₁₆-inch heavy-point tip. The #S tip gives a softer edge and can be used for all degrees of darkness, including "black." He used the sharp tip to outline the Celtic knots in the gourd by that name.

Carousel Rhinoceros

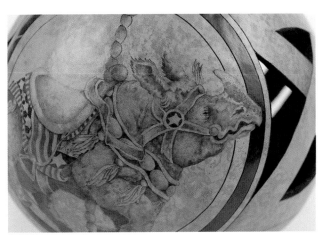

Carousel Rhinoceros detail.

Flower Circle

Carousel Rhinoceros, back side (Celtic knots)

ARTIST THEODORE ROYBAL

BURNING TOOL
Detail Master IV, #1C angle-blade, #2C round, #7C ¼-inch, and #7A ⅛-inch round tips

The artist chose to place the sketch where dark marks were already on the gourd or to shade to cover flaws. He lightly sanded the surface to smooth out unwanted lumps and to lighten dark spots.

Nautilus detail

Elk

Indian

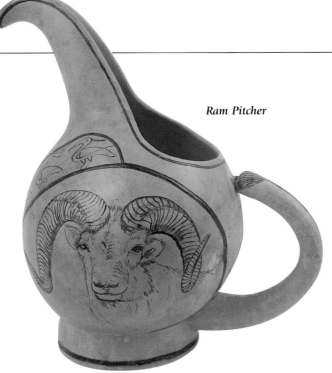

Ram Pitcher

Sheep

Eagle

ARTIST HAL HALL

BURNING TOOL
Dremel Versatip wood burner,
"V" tip

Using the "V" tip, artist Hal Hall
burns in his design and shades in
the background with the side of
the tip.

Autumn Leaves

Barn

ARTIST PAT GRIGG

BURNING TOOL
Walnut Hollow Farm's Creative Wood Burner
950°F, #5991 mini-universal point

Pat Grigg uses the Walnut Hollow Farm 950°F
wood burner with the mini-universal point to
create elegant gourds like these decorative floral
bowls. The scalloped open top takes on petal
shapes.

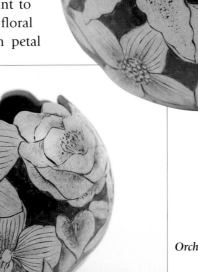

*Lily and
Dogwood Blossoms*

Orchids

ARTIST BEV ROBBINS

BURNING TOOL
Hot Tool, standard and round
tips

The artist Bev Robbins created
Hide and Seek with two gourds,
using the Hot Tool and standard
and round tips. A fish swims
through marine plants.

Hide and Seek

ARTIST GRETCHEN CETERAS

BURNING TOOL
Hot Tool, standard tip; sunlight

Artist Gretchen Ceteras burns the design by focusing the sun's rays, a source of heat, on the gourd. See her finished Poppies and Rattle gourds. She used solar heat for the heavy parallel lines on the Friends gourd. She also burns whole gourd, like the Rattle.

She also creates other gourd artwork, like that of the Anemone, with a hot tool. Notice how the defects in a gourd can add texture or a three-dimensional look to a design.

The magnifying glass helps focus the sun's rays to burn the desired design.

Anemone

Magnolia Flower

Small, apple-shaped container with lid

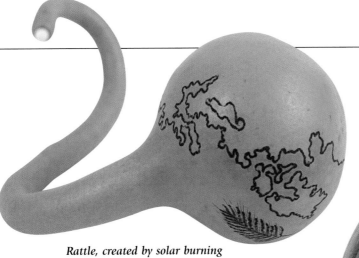

Rattle, created by solar burning

The defects in this gourd give texture to the leaves and flower.

Poppies, created by solar burning

Friends, front and back of same gourd.
The heavy lines were solar burned.

ARTIST KATHY RIKER

BURNING TOOL
Detail Master, #1A, #1C, #7B, #9A, #9C, #10A, #10B, #10C, #12A tips

For the Power of the Great Spirit gourd, the artist Kathy Riker uses the #1A pyrography pen to first outline parts of the body and other features.

With short strokes of the #10A pen, she created feathers on the head and shading around the eye and beak. Riker chose the #12A pen to create the circle for the eye and circles in the wing below the American Indian face. She used the #10B tip for medium strokes to create feathers on the chest, and the #10C tip for thin longer lines for feathers on the lower wing.

Fish-scale pens #9A and #9C drew the feet. The #7B pen helped shade the face, feet, and under each feather before she created the actual feather lines. By moving the pen in circles, she could create light and dark effects. Using a #7B pen, she shaded around the Indian's face. She drew the face lines with a #1A tip.

Riker also drew the outline of the whole tree and ends of branches with the #1A tip. She used short lines to create the curving effect of the branches. The #1C pen cut the thicker, bold lines into the tree. The #10C pen for thin lines mixed with the #1A pen helped create knots and the curved effect. The #7B pen helped create the shading before and after she drew lines with the #1A, #1C and #10C.

Zenith, Power of the Great Spirit

Zenith, detail of the American Indian face and the eagle's feathers, created with still tinier feathers.

Zenith, detail on the back

ARTIST JILL WALKER

BURNING TOOLS
Detail Master, #1A, #2A, and #6A tips; Micro-Torch

For the well-seasoned gourd, which was quite hard, Jill Walker used her Detail Master, applying most lines with the #1A tip.

Small dots for fine shading on the woman's dress that show through her cloak were created with a #6A tip at a fairly low temperature. For heavier shading, she used a #2A tip.

For scorching, Walker used the Micro-Torch fueled by butane. It allows you to adjust the flame size and temperature, and its piezo-electric ignition makes it convenient to turn off and on as needed. This also reduces the danger of accidental burns. Walker used templates made from several layers of heavy-duty aluminum foil to help direct areas for scorching.

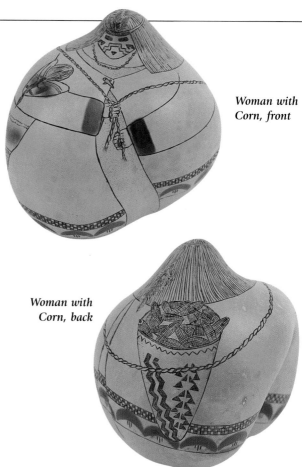

Woman with Corn, front

Woman with Corn, back

ARTIST JEANNE CHAPMAN

BURNING TOOL
Hot Tool, standard tip

Gourd artist Jeanne Chapman uses all sides of the tip. She pushes it up and turns it upside down as necessary to create a variety of textures.

Hawaiian gourd with sailing ship and bird

ARTIST CAROL WALKER

BURNING TOOLS
Walnut Hollow, model #5593; Creative Wood burner, various tips

For line detail, artist Carol Walker uses a wedge-shaped tip. A spatula-shaped tip creates shading for flowers and other objects. Walker uses various other tips for stippling flowers, symbols, paw prints, and dots.

Wolf

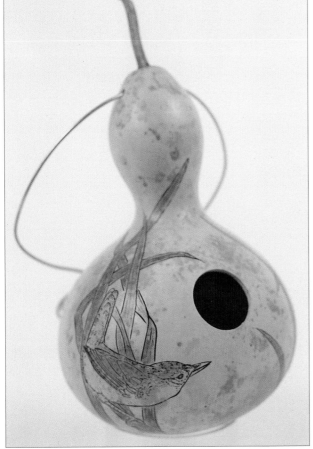

Wren Birdhouse

ARTIST CARLOTTA BRANDENBURG

BURNING TOOL
Detail Master IV wood burner, solid tip burner

Artist Carlotta Brandenburg used a standard hobby-style wood burner for her Duck creation. She added curling feathers to the mouth of her Duck container. For the Wren Birdhouse gourd she used the Detail Master. The gourd hole bored near the center, ready for a bird, like the wren depicted, to enter. Of course, a real bird probably wouldn't choose this gourd for a nest. The copper wire allows you to hang it for decoration.

Duck

ARTIST DARIENNE MCAULEY

BURNING TOOL
Colwood Detailer, model #2001, heavy-duty cord, #S and #H tips

For Wolves at Sunset, artist Darienne McAuley maintained the #S angled stencil tip at red-hot temperature and applied pressure to deep-burn texture on the hills and shoreline. The shoreline served as a dam to separate dye colors. McAuley burned trees with the #S tip and burned wolves lightly with the #H tip, using both the point and the flat side.

For the petroglyphs, the artist used the #C tip red hot while applying pressure to create deeply burned indentations corresponding to pictures chiseled and gouged into rock. McAuley also used a homemade burning chamber made from a large wooden box with a bathroom-vent fan attached to draw smoke away and out of the artist's studio. She attached a dryer hose to a duct through her studio window.

Petroglyphs

Wolves at Sunset

ARTIST ALEX (NÄ-VÄ-CHE) VILLALVA

BURNING TOOL
Detail Master II Sabre, #1A and
#7B tips

Natural resins in the gourd produce the glossy surface of the shaded areas. Villalva outlines and burns deep lines for strands of hair with the #1A tip. He shades dark areas with the #7B tip.

On the artist's three gourds, the stylized hummingbird maiden sings to the hummingbird. The corn god and corn maiden appear in a spiritual corn dance. And the butterfly gourd tells the Papago American Indian nation's creation story of how butterflies came into being.

*Papago Story of
Butterfly Creation*

Hummingbird Maiden, front and back

Corn God and Corn Maiden

ARTIST RONNA WUTTKE

BURNING TOOL
Colwood Super Pro II, #S tip; Walnut Hollow
Farm wood burners, #MC.030, #MC, and bullet-
head tips

Ronna Wuttke uses the sharpest point for detailing
and outlining. For light shading and a golden burn,
Wuttke turns the wood burner on at low wattage and
uses a bullet-head tip. The #MC.030 tip is good for
detailing and producing darker burns, such as outlining trees. The #MC tip outlines and creates the
darkest shades of bark. For depth, produce several
hues or colors, the artist advises.

With the bullet-head tip, Wuttke went over the
whole tree and dark bark. The #S tip on both high- and
low-heat settings was used to shade large areas. For
intricate work on the bulkhead and church, she used a
filed-down tip from the Walnut Hollow burner -
assortment.

Grandfather's Past

Nordic Bowl front

Nordic Bowl back

ARTIST KIMO TRUEMAN

BURNING TOOL
Detail Master, Sabre IV, #3A, #5A, and #7C tips

First artist Kimo Trueman sketches his design on the gourd; then he burns it in with the #5A pen. Using a high-speed rotary tool, he carves away some of the gourd's surface for depth and uses the #7C pen for shadowing. Finally, he uses the #3A pen for fine lines and edging to create a three-dimensional look.

His Hibiscus has four buds. The men's jewelry box has a feather band on the bowl and buckeyes for legs, and bears a Hawaiian sea eagle on its top.

Men's jewelry box

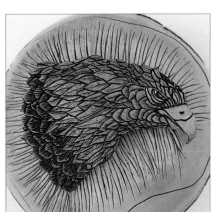

Top of men's jewelry box

Hibiscus

ARTIST SUSAN SWEET

BURNING TOOL
Razertip, #1S, #5M, #9S tips

Susan Sweet creates colorful bowls, jars, and masks in various shapes. To find out how she creates these works, see pages 52 to 53.

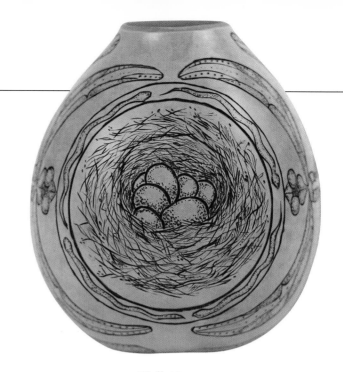

Bird's Nest

Kingfisher gourd and detail

Painted Lioness

Mask

Dragonfly Bowl, side and top views

ARTIST DYAN MAI PETERSON

BURNING TOOL
Detail Master, #1C pen

The #1C pen can be turned on its side for all kinds of effects, and the point can be used for stippling. The artist Dyan Mai Peterson taught herself to experiment with the pen, holding it in all different directions.

Houses at the Dock

Hawk Bowl

ARTIST ORCHID DAVIS

BURNING TOOL
Colwood Detailer, #J tip

When creating the Hawk and Horse bowls, the artist Orchid Davis used flowing curves drawn with the #J pen and cutouts. She advises that when burning cutouts, don't try to burn through in one stroke. "Just keep slicing with fairly high heat until you cut through. Too much heat will set the gourd on fire," Davis says.

Horse Bowl

ARTIST SHARON BOYD

BURNING TOOLS
Walnut Hollow wood burner, #5590 universal
and #5591 universal tips; Wall Lenk Decorative
Branding Tool, #WB24KT all-purpose decor-brand
tip and #DB303 circle-brand tip

"Instead of pre-drawing my designs, I wood-burn the
perimeters and then fill in the spaces with designs
that please me. I like curvilinear forms, using straight
lines for contrast. I am finished when I run out of
space. I find pyroengraving mesmerizing. I like sharp
tips for fine line work," Boyd says.

Ebony Bottle-Neck

ARTIST RIMONA GALE

BURNING TOOL
Hot Tool

Artist Rimona Gale advises using
little scratchy back-and-forth movements with the Hot Tool standard
tip to create shading.

She carefully measures and
sketches out her geometric patterns before burning

*To create shading, make little scratchy
back–and-forth movements with the tip.*

Zigzag Jar

ARTIST DUANE TEETER

BURNING TOOL
Hot Tool, standard tip

Duane Teeter does all his work with the Hot Tool, using the standard tip in a variety of ways, creating these elegant designs. He demonstrates his techniques step by step earlier in this chapter, pages 30 to 42.

Faces

Geometrics

Bird-Head Abstract

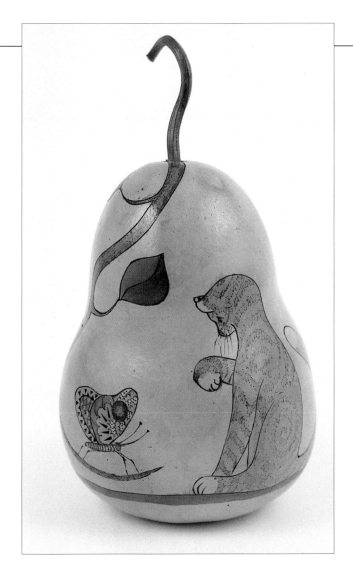

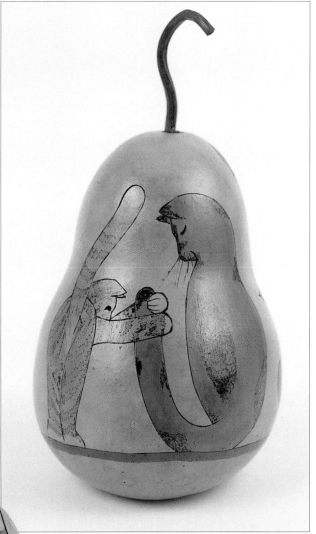

Cat Tails, two sides

Petal Abstract

Gourd Jewelry

*M*any artists have specialized in creating gourd jewelry, often by taking advantage of the natural earth tones of the gourds and a rich black or brown design. Here are Carolyn Rushton, Robin McBride Scott, Vera Kuttig, Pat Wilkinson, Carol Morrison, and Orchid Davis's jewelry designs. They've created a variety of gourd pins, pendants, necklaces, and earrings. Many earring designs can also double as cufflink designs.

If you fashion men's cufflinks or other jewelry, you may find Kimo Trueman's men's jewelry boxes on page 111 useful additions to your gourd repertoire.

For gourd jewelry, many techniques are the same as for other gourd artwork, but the artist works on a smaller scale, perhaps with more attention to detail. You'll be able to make more than a single piece of jewelry from a large gourd. Gourd jewelry allows you to show off your gourd creations to a larger public.

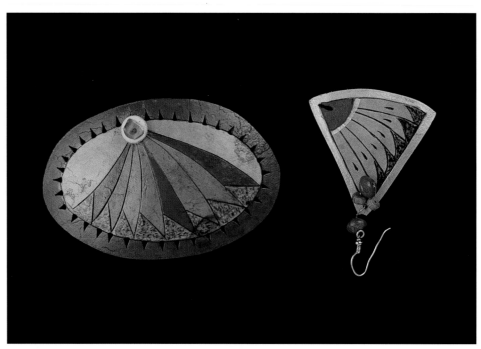

Earrings and pin. Jewelry design by Vera Kuttig.

ARTIST VERA KUTTIG

BURNING TOOL
Hot Tool, standard chisel tip

Vera Kuttig varies the pressure and how long she leaves the tip on the gourd's surface to create the design on her gourd pendants, earrings, and pins.

Necklace

Necklace with matching earrings

Necklace

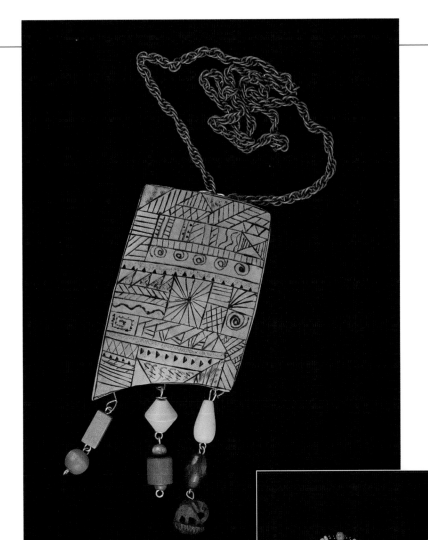

Necklaces

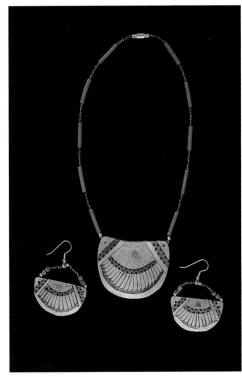

Necklaces with matching earrings

VERA KUTTIG'S
JEWELRY DESIGNS

GOURD JEWELRY BASICS

ARTIST CAROLYN RUSHTON

BURNING TOOLS
Detail Master IV Sabre, #1A tip;
Razertip, #1S and #5S tips

Here's how, step-by-step, artist Carolyn Rushton creates a gourd-shaped pendant with shaded gourd designs.

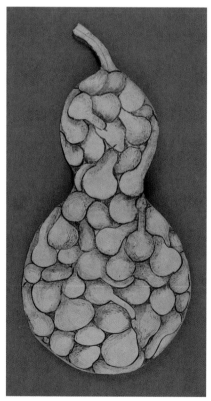

Gourd Pendant or Pin

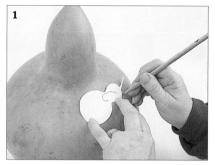

Use a pencil and a template to draw a design on the gourd. The template has to be an appropriate size and design to create your own personal gourd jewelry.

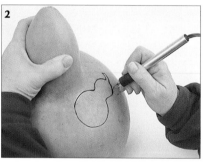

Use the Detail Master IV #1A pen to cut out the gourd piece for your pendant, earring, pin, or other piece of jewelry.

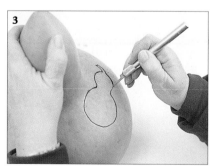

Instead of the Detail Master pen, you may prefer to use an X-acto knife with a #15 saw blade to cut out the gourd piece.

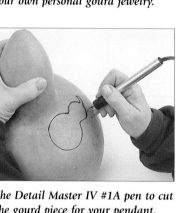

Gourd stencil or template cutout

With the sanding wheel of the Minicraft or other high-speed rotary tool, smooth the back of the gourd piece that you cut out.

Caution: Wear a dust mask during this process to keep from inhaling gourd dust; some people are allergic to this dust.

5

Draw the image you desire on the gourd piece with a pencil.

6

Use a Razertip #5S short spear to burn over the pencil lines.

7

Use the Razertip #1S pen to shade the image and to separate the individual images from each other in the design. Shade to produce "roundness" or three-dimensionality to each individual gourd shape in your design.

CAROLYN RUSHTON'S JEWELRY DESIGNS

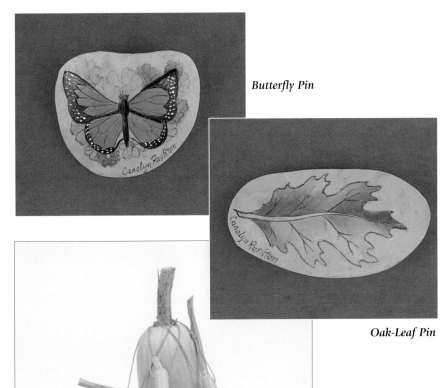

Butterfly Pin

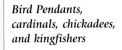

Oak-Leaf Pin

Bird Pendants, cardinals, chickadees, and kingfishers

ARTIST PAT WILKINSON

Artist Pat Wilkinson used multiple pieces of a gourd to create this necklace, which she strung together with thin wire, cord, and brown and beige beads.

ARTIST CAROL MORRISON

Here are six pairs of earrings with geometric designs. Artist Carol Morrison also creates larger works but likes the idea of wearable art.

Earrings

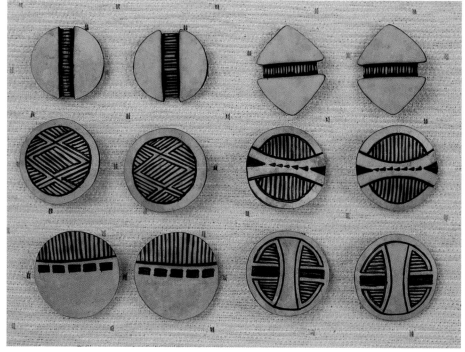

ARTIST CAROL ST. PIERRE

Carol St. Pierre uses the Hot Tool with the standard tip for most of
her work. Occasionally she will use a circle tip on the Hot Tool.

Necklaces

ARTIST ROBIN MCBRIDE SCOTT

For Celtic knot work, Robin McBride Scott uses the pointed end of the angled spade tip to do line drawing.

Celtic Knot-Work Pins

Celtic Design Necklace

Celtic Knot-Work Pins

Pen Photo	Description	Razertip	Leisure Time's Detail Master	Colwood	Nibsburner
	³⁄₁₆-inch round end blade	2M	2-C	D ³⁄₁₆-inch round ³⁄₁₆-inch S shading	2B
	³⁄₃₂-inch round tip	2S		special order	2C
	¼-inch angled round tip	HD2LC	7-C	special order	
	³⁄₁₆-inch angled round tip	HD2MC	7-B	special order	
	⅛-inch angled round tip	HD2SC	7-A	special order	
	⁹⁄₃₂-inch flat skew	4L			
	³⁄₁₆-inch flat skew	4M			
	⁷⁄₃₂-inch spear	5M		E ¼-inch spade	

Pen Photo	Description	Razertip	Leisure Time's Detail Master	Colwood	Nibsburner
	³/₃₂-inch spear	5S		F ³/₁₆-inch spear	5
	blunt curved ⁷/₃₂-inch spear 2 sides	5HDMC			
	spear blade 2 sides	HD5M	5-A		
	spear blade extra long 2½-inch	#5X2 (2 inch) #5X3 (3 inch)	5-AX (2½ inch)		
	¼-inch chisel	6L		special order	
	½-inch chisel	6LW		special order	
	⁵/₃₂-inch chisel	6M		special order	
	⅛-inch chisel; also calligraphy	6S	6-B	SQ ³/₃₂-inch square	
	¼-inch angled square end blade	HD6MC	4-C	¼-inch square angled	

Pen Photo	Description	Razertip	Leisure Time's Detail Master	Colwood	Nibsburner
	⅛-inch angled square end blade	HD6SC	4-A	⅛-inch square angled	
	³⁄₁₆-inch angled square end blade		4-B		
	⁵⁄₁₆-inch round skew	7L			KN1
	⁷⁄₃₂-inch round skew	7M		F ³⁄₁₆-inch spear	K2
	⅛-inch round skew	7S		PS	KN3
	¼-inch burnishing tip	8			1DR
	¹⁄₁₆-inch writing tip	9	6-A	C writing tip	4
	¹⁄₁₆-inch writing tip with point	9S		MC.030	
	general Pyro L	10L			
	general Pyro R	10R			

Pen Photo	Description	Razertip	Leisure Time's Detail Master	Colwood	Nibsburner
	2-line pen	#11-2			
	9/32-inch curved spear	12L			
	curved spear	12S			
	¼-inch rounded knife blade	HD14L	10-C	BR	
	3/16-inch rounded knife blade	14M	10-B	GR, HR	
	⅛-inch rounded knife blade		10-A		
	⅛-inch rounded knife blade extra long		10-AXL		
	⅛-inch thin skew with round heel	14S	3-A	M	
	quill maker	15L			1CR

Pen Photo	Description	Razertip	Leisure Time's Detail Master	Colwood	Nibsburner
	quill maker	15LH			1CL
	¼-inch angled round with point for shading corners	HD16L	8-C	special order	
	³⁄₁₆-inch angled round with point for shading corners	HD16M	8-B	special order	
	⅛-inch angled round with point for shading from corners	HD16S	8-A	special order	
	versatile	18L			
	versatile	18XL			
	versatile	18M			
	versatile	18S			
	versatile	18XS			

Pen Photo	Description	Razertip	Leisure Time's Detail Master	Colwood	Nibsburner
	fish scale full scale varies in size to order	20.06D	9-E. 9-F	1+1, 1-6, 15	
	fish scale half scale varies in size to order	20.06R		FSS, FSM, FSL	
	fish scale lateral line tip	F25		8, 9, 2+2, 14	
	fish scale full scale sharp "smile" varies in size to order	29.06R	9-C, 9-D	special order	fish tips
	fish scale full scale blunt "smile" varies in size to order	29.06D		special order	
	3/16-inch spoon	HD30M		special order	
	1/8-inch spoon	HD30S		special order	
	ball burnisher			11, 12, 13	

Pen Description	Razertip	Leisure Time's Detail Master	Colwood	Nibsburner
circle tips			R(SM) $\frac{3}{32}$ inch, R(LG) $\frac{3}{16}$ inch	
double round			DA	
double point			DG	
$\frac{1}{8}$-inch thin skewer with round heel extra 2½ inches long		3-AXL		
$\frac{3}{16}$-inch, $\frac{1}{8}$-inch, $\frac{3}{32}$-inch circle pen		12 A-C		
teardrop pen copper		12-D		
square-end shading pen copper		12-E		
wedge-shape, knife-edge copper		12-F		

Solid-Core Pyrographic Tools & Tips

Tip Photo	M.M. Newman's Hot Tool	Janik Ltd.
	standard skew chisel tip	#21 universal
	needle tip	#22 needle
	feather tip	
	signature tip (stencil tip)	
	button tip	
	knife tip (shading tip)	
	¹⁄₁₆-inch circle tip	
	⅛-inch circle tip	C23 3-mm circle
	³⁄₁₆-inch circle tip	C24 4-mm circle

Tip Photo	M.M. Newman's Hot Tool	Janik Ltd.
	¹⁄₁₆-inch round tip (¹⁄₁₆-inch dot)	
	⅛-inch round tip (⅛-inch dot)	E23 3mm disc
	³⁄₁₆-inch round tip (³⁄₁₆-inch dot, also called blank)	E24 4mm disc
	LM broad writing tip	B22 2mm ball
	LM fine writing tip	B21 1mm ball
	44 line multi-groove tip	
	56 line multi-groove tip	
	bent shading tip	P20 filling in or #23 flat
	transfer tip	

Nichrome Wire Pyroengraving Tools

Manufacturers of Nichrome wire tools sell spools of nichrome wire for making your own custom nibs (tips), as well as selling premade wire nibs for their pens.

Photo	Pyrographic Equipment Manufacturing	Janik Ltd.
	20, 22, 24 gauge pointed nib	23, 25 gauge
	20, 22, 24 gauge shading nib	23, 25 gauge
	20, 22, 24 gauge calligraphy nib	23, 25 gauge "spoon point"

METRIC EQUIVALENTS

1/32 inch = 0.08 centimeters = 0.8 millimeters
1/16 inch = 0.16 centimeters = 1.6 millimeters
1/8 inch = 0.32 centimeters = 3.2 millimeters
1/4 inch = 0.63 centimeters = 6.3 millimeters
1/2 inch = 1.25 centimeters = 12.5 millimeters
3/4 inch = 1.9 centimeters = 19 millimeters
1 inch = 2.54 centimeters

1 foot = 30 centimeters
39 inches = 1 meter
1 cup = 8 fluid ounces = 240 milliliters
2 cups = 1 pint = 0.45 liter
4 cups = 2 pints = 1 quart = 0.89 liter
2 quarts = 1.9 liters
4 quarts = 1 gallon = 3.8 liters

Temperature Conversions
Fahrenheit to Centigrade (Celsius)
(Fahrenheit degrees − 32) x 5/9 = Centigrade degrees
Centigrade (Celsius) to Fahrenheit
(Centigrade degrees x 9/5) + 32 = Fahrenheit degrees

SUPPLY SOURCES

Gourd Seeds
Suzanne Ashworth
5007 Del Rio Rd.
Sacramento, CA 95822-2514

Rocky Ford Gourds
c/o Kern Ackerman
178 Losee St., Box 222
Cygnet, OH 43413

Gourds
Glen Burkhalter
Dried Gourds
153 Wiljoy Rd.
Lacey's Spring, AL 35754

Dalton Farms
610 CR 336
Piggott, AR 72454

The Gourd Factory
P.O. Box 9
Linden, CA 95236

The Gourd Farm
c/o Lena Braswell
Route 1, Box 73
Wrens, GA 30833

Randy Harelson
Gourd Garden and Curiosity Shop
4808 E Country Rd. 30-A
Santa Rosa Beach, FL 32459

Tom Keller
P.O. Box 1115
West Point, MS 39773

Ozark Country Creations
Dennis and Becky Hatfield
30226 Holly Rd.
Pierce City, MO 65723

The Pumpkin and Gourd Farm
101 Creston Rd.
Paso Robles, CA 93446

Helen Thomas
Sandlady's Gourd Farm
Rural Route 4, Box 86
Tangier, IN 47952

Tree Mover and Gourd Farm
5014 E Avenue N
Palmdale, CA 93552

Doug and Sue Welburn
40787 Deluz Murrieta Rd.
Fallbrook, CA 92028

West Mountain Gourd Farm
Route 1, Box 853
Gilmer, TX 75644

Zittel's Gourd Farm
6781 Oak Ave.
Folsom, CA 95630

John Van Tol
P.O. Box 298
East Maitland, NSW 2323
Australia

American Gourd Society
317 Maple Court
Kokomo, IN 46902-3633

Wood-Burning Tools
M. M. Newman Corp
Hot Tools Division
24 Tioga Way
Marblehead, MA 01945

Razertip Industries, Inc.
P.O. Box 1258
Martensville, SK S0K 2T0
Canada

Pyrographic Equipment
Manufacturing,
P.O. Box 331
Kilsyth, Victoria 3137
Australia

Colwood Electronics
15 Meridian Rd.
Eatontown, NJ 07724

Nibsburner
3255 Blue Mountain Way
Colorado Springs, CO 80906

Leisure Time Products, Inc.
2650 Davisson St.
River Grove, IL 60171

Wall Lenk Corporation
P.O. Box 3349
Kinston, NC 28501

Walnut Hollow Farm
1409 State Rd. 23
Dodgeville, WI 53533

Ardith Willner
24 Clubhouse Rd.
Santa Cruz, CA 95060

The Caning Shop
926 Gilman St.
Berkeley, CA 94710-1494
1-800-544-3373
www.caning.com

Janik Ltd
Brickfield Lane, Ruthin
Denbigshire, North Wales LL15 2TN

Peter Child Woodturning Supplies
The Old Hyde
Little Yeldham, Near Halstead
Essex CO9 4QT
Great Britain

INDEX

For more books on gourd crafts, look for Ginger Summit and Jim Widess's The *Complete Book of Gourd Craft* (Lark Books, 1996); Ginger Summit's *Gourds in Your Garden* (Sterling, 2000); Ginger Summit's *Gourd Crafts: 20 Weekend Projects* (Lark Books, 1999); Ginger Summit and Jim Widess's *Making Gourd Musical Instruments* (Sterling, 1999); and Betty Auth's *Wood-Burning: 20 Great-Looking Projects to Decorate in a Weekend* (Lark Books, 1999).